CHRISTIAN MATURITY

Applying God's Principles for Spiritual Growth

Dr. Lester Hutson

Christian Maturity: Applying God's Principles for Spiritual Growth

ISBN: 978-0-9836802-7-7

www.lesterhutson.org

Dedication

My mother was Dena Grimes Hutson. I do not have the ability to put into words what an impact this godly woman had on my life. She was very poor and not highly educated, but I can't imagine a godlier and more caring person. I was the last of four children, seven years behind my lovely sister Janie. Mom invested in me. I didn't recognize or appreciate it at the time, but her purity and commitment to God was rubbing off onto me. No human has ever molded and made me more of who I am than Dena Grimes Hutson. There were others, but she was the playmaker. Her fingerprints are the predominate ones all over me. I cannot remember her ever teaching me even one formal lesson, but teach me she did: integrity, honesty, love for God and His Word, respect for other people and their property, honor for father and mother, a work ethic, giving, forgiving, morality and this list could go on for a very long time. The lessons were routine and on-going. She more than any other was my guide, my mentor, that person who gave me stability and direction.

Mother was killed in a car wreck when I was 16. I had been *born again* into the family of God when I was 13, and before my next birthday I had publicly committed my life to the gospel ministry. The trauma of mother's death took its toll; and as a young person and as a *babe in Christ*, I was struggling. I had lots of desire and zeal (and hurt) but very little direction. About that time Kermit Johnson stepped into my life. He reached out to me and stayed there for the next three decades. We never lived close together or spent long hours together, but he was there when I needed him. He took time to answer my questions, challenge my thinking and even kick me real hard in the seat of my pants. He was honest with me, even when I didn't like it. When I fell flat on my face, he sought me out and wouldn't let me *suck my thumb*. He's been in heaven a long time, but Kermit Johnson still ministers to me. So many times I have relived his answers and reconsidered his counsel. At times he's like an inner voice speaking to me. In addition to what he said to me, his example was (and is) powerful. He wasn't perfect, but he was a good man. He was mature. I saw it! He was for real, not just a *hot-shot* who put on a good show. Like my dear mother, Kermit was in the dark what he was in the light. That gave him a pulpit with me. Along with my mother, I bear his fingerprints on my soul.

It is with great respect and honor that I dedicate this book to my precious mother, Dena Grimes Hutson and to my friend forever, Kermit Johnson. In them I had the wonderful experience of seeing two fully mature Christians up close and personal.

Dena Grimes Hutson

Kermit Johnson

Table of Contents

Foreword

Full maturity does not equate with perfection. There are no perfect people, but there are people who are fully mature. All of them could be better, but by any standard they are adults. God wants you to grow up to full age in Him. That's not a *pipe dream*; it can happen in you. This book is about getting there, about moving from a babe in Christ to a mature spiritual adult.

I am now well passed *threescore and ten.* Through the years it has been my observation that there are not nearly as many spiritually mature people as there should be. I have also observed that there is a great deal of confusion about what spiritual maturity is and about how to distinguish really mature people from counterfeits. It is my deep desire that this little book will bring much understanding and clarity to this subject.

I realize there is the risk that some may misuse the information found here and become judges. God forbid! May this information cause you to take a very honest and objective look at yourself, not others! Please do not use it to analyze and pass judgment on all of the people in your life.

May it also make you wiser and less susceptible to deception! This book can help you go for gold and not *fool's gold.* Once you see what true maturity is and how it manifests itself, you will not be easily deceived and *taken in* by pretenders. In part, it was such wide-spread misunderstanding and confusion with its consequent damage to the cause of our great God that motivated me to write this book.

The expectation of healthy growth to maturity underlies life. Parents want it for their children and God wants it for His spiritual children. In both the physical and the spiritual worlds failure of proper growth and development is regarded as a most serious malady. It is my prayer that this book will result in new growth in you. May it also equip you to promote healthy spiritual growth in those around you!

Lester Hutson

DEFINING MATURITY

Chapter 1

Maturity: More than Immediately Meets the Eye

Jake is big, strong and over 50 years old. From a physical standpoint, he's *mature* in most ways; however, those around Jake know better. Jake is mentally handicapped, a five year old in a fifty year old body! Jake knows something is wrong, but he can't figure it out. It's a sad picture.

MATURE

Webster says *mature* means "fully grown or developed." Thus *maturity* is "the condition of being fully grown or developed." [1] But what about *Jake?* Obviously, he's *fully developed,* brain and all; but something is badly wrong. His mental development didn't keep up with his physical development. He's grown, but he's not mature. Sometimes people like Jake have to be kept in special homes; they call them homes for mentally handicapped children. *Children?* Yes, they're grown, but they are not mature. They're still *children.* Maturity in people is not determined exclusively by the age or size of the body. Maturity demands a fully developed body and mind.

Immaturity is not limited to the young in age or those with mental handicaps. What about the guy who is thirty with a fully grown body and no mental handicap? He's a playboy into himself who assumes no responsibility. His word is no good, he's hotheaded, not dependable as a worker or to relationships and he doesn't take care of his wife or children. Most of his decisions lack wisdom or depth in thinking. An example of this is a man named Buster. He's over sixty, smart, handsome and has a well-developed, grown body. He's not handicapped physically or mentally. He's a great photographer, can carry on a very intelligent conversation and has had a parade of great opportunities; however, Buster will not do his work and has lost one good job after another. He's irresponsible and a recluse living in a pigsty; at times a street person. By choice! Could such a one be rightfully called a mature adult? He's not like *Jake,* but he still hasn't grown up. By almost any social measure of maturity, Buster is an immature old man.

Yet, maturity certainly doesn't mean *without flaw* or *perfect* in the sense of beyond improvement. A mature ear of corn may be dwarfed, bug-stung and quite inferior; and all mature people have flaws and could use much improvement.

There's an innate complexity in maturity; however, mature people stand out. As children grow up, signs of maturity begin to appear both physically and spiritually. The body develops, but so do emotions, behavior and thinking. Thought processes move to a deeper more responsible level and a greater sense of responsibility develops. They increasingly respond to the realities of life in a more positive way and their lives are characterized by fewer and fewer childish traits.

Part of the concept of maturity is realizing the potential of what you were intended and designed to be and do. It's progress beyond the formative stages to a point of fruitfulness. A mature person is still not *getting it all together*, but has *gotten enough of it together* to function effectively at the task for which he was intended.

GROWTH

Growth is beautiful. It's difficult to adequately describe the growth of a little child: to see the little legs, fingers and body get bigger and bigger, to see the coordination ever sharpen, to watch him put a bite into his own mouth, to watch his face light up and hear him say, "I did it myself." How glorious to see evidences that his little mind is growing every day: the little hand waving *bye-bye*, the spontaneous smile when he sees you, the outstretched arms when grandpa walks into the daycare.

God is very interested in this issue of *maturity,* and He addressed it at length in His Word, the Bible. The idea of growth to maturity is His idea and observable throughout the natural world: old, mature, reproducing trees and animals. He equipped the world for reproduction. His first command was *"Be fruitful, and multiply, and replenish the earth, and subdue it,"* **Genesis 1:28**. Physical reproduction demands a great degree of physical maturity and is a sign of it. Inherent in the plan of God is growth to maturity. The cycle of life is dependent upon it.

When a person trusts Jesus Christ as personal Savior he is *"born again,"* **1 Peter 1:23**, and thus spiritually becomes a *"newborn babe,"* **1 Peter 2:2**. And what is God's plan for *newborn babes*? Growth! Start immediate growth! *"As newborn babes, desire the sincere milk of the word, that ye may grow thereby"* **1 Peter 2:2**. The Greek word for *"grow"* is <u>auxano</u> meaning to enlarge, increase, grow up. Jesus not only grew physically, **Luke 1:80**, but also *"the child grew, and waxed strong in spirit, filled with wisdom: and the grace of God was upon him,"* **Luke 2:40**. Believers are God's spiritual children whom He expects to become stabilized in His doctrine and practice. We are not to be *"children, tossed to and fro, and carried about with every wind of doctrine, by the sleight of men, and cunning craftiness, whereby they lie in wait to deceive; But speaking the truth in love, may grow up in him in all things, which is the head, even Christ,"* **Ephesians 4:14-15**. He thus instructs His children to *"grow in grace, and in the knowledge of our Lord and Saviour Jesus Christ,"* **2 Peter 3:18**.

BABES

Birth defects! Thank God for the wonderful parents who give such special love and care to a handicapped child, but most parents pray their child will be born whole in both body and mind. Children born with physical or mental defects can't help it. Prevention is not within their power. That is not the case in the realm of spiritual children. Nobody is *born again* with a spiritual birth defect. Yet many of God's children are spiritually deformed, slow, old in years but functioning far below their age. While they should be grown up, they are not; still *babes* in the spiritual sense of the word; old, but no maturity.

There are two words in the Greek language of the New Testament that translate *babes* or *children* into English. One is <u>brephos</u>. It's the word used to speak of newborn babies and even young children. Before John the Baptist was born of Elizabeth, *"the babe leaped in her womb,"* **Luke 1:41,44**. Paul used <u>brephos</u> in reference to young Timothy. *"And that from a child thou hast known the holy scriptures, which are able to make thee wise unto salvation through faith which is in Christ Jesus"* **2 Timothy 3:15**. It's the word to denote a whole, healthy baby or young child.

The other word is <u>nepios</u>. This word denotes people who are old enough to show signs of maturity, but who are thinking and behaving like little babies or children. It is not a compliment to be called a <u>nepios</u>. The idea is quite obvious in **Hebrews 5:11-14**. *"Of whom we have many things to say, and hard to be uttered, seeing ye are dull of hearing. For when for the time ye ought to be teachers, ye have need that one teach you again which be the first principles of the oracles of God; and are become such as have need of milk, and not of strong meat. For every one that useth milk is unskilful in the word of righteousness: for he is a babe. But strong meat belongeth to them that are of full age, even those who by reason of use have their senses exercised to discern both good and evil."* God's spiritual children ought to grow up and begin thinking and behaving like adults. The Corinthians Christians were notorious for division, pride, sex sins, abuse of spiritual blessings and a host of other undisciplined, immature and godless activities. In his first letter to them, Paul addressed them as *"babes"* (nepios), *"And I, brethren, could not speak unto you as unto spiritual, but as unto carnal, even as unto babes in Christ. I have fed you with milk, and not with meat: for hitherto ye were not able to bear it, neither yet now are ye able. For ye are yet carnal: for whereas there is among you envying, and strife, and divisions, are ye not carnal, and walk as men?"* **1 Corinthians 3:1-3**. Paul said, *"When I was a child, I spake as a child, I understood as a child, I thought as a child: but when I became a man, I put away childish things,"* **1 Corinthians 13:11**.

God expects that of every one of His spiritual children. The condition of growth to maturity in a Christian sense is called *spirituality.* The Bible refers to such ones as *spiritual.* The Greek word is pneumatikos. *"Ye which are spiritual"* (hoi pneumatikoi) is a reference to spiritual grownups. Greek scholar A.T. Robertson calls them "The spiritually led, the spiritual experts in mending souls." [2] They are *"them that are of full age, even those who by reason of use have their senses exercised to discern both good and evil,"* **Hebrews 5:14**. Reports of spiritual maturity in the believers in Colosse reached Paul. The report reached him through *"a faithful minister of Christ"* named *Epaphras "who also declared unto us your love in the Spirit. For this cause we also, since the day we heard it, do not cease to pray for you, and to desire that ye might be filled with the knowledge of his will in all wisdom and spiritual understanding; That ye might walk worthy of the Lord unto all pleasing, being fruitful in every good work, and increasing in the knowledge of God; Strengthened with all might, according to his glorious power, unto all patience and longsuffering with joyfulness; Giving thanks unto the Father, which hath made us meet to be partakers of the inheritance of the saints in light,"* **Colossians 1:8-12**.

A normal childhood is a delightful time, but it is heartbreaking to watch a child fall behind especially in mental development. A spiritually underdeveloped baby is not a pretty sight: all of the sibling rivalries, the selfish *it's all about me* attitude, the thumb-sucking and pouting, the bullying, the divisive spirit. King David spoke of *"the grass upon the housetops, which withereth afore it groweth up,"* **Psalm 129:6**. What a picture of many Christians! They stopped growing before they got grown. What a toll this takes on the Lord's churches where they are; and the more there are of these childish adults in a church, the greater the hindrance to the work of God. The church in Corinth is a case in point.

In the family of God there are no birth defects. After sufficient time for growth, all who continue to think and behave like children do so by their own choice. A stunted, under-developed spiritual condition cannot be blamed on God.

STATUS CHECK

What is your status? Are you a child of God? If so, where do you fit in the picture? Are you a spiritual brephos, one who is newly saved and whose spiritual growth is indicative of your spiritual age? Are you a spiritual nepios, one whose spiritual thinking and behavior is far below your spiritual age? Hopefully you are pneumatikos, spiritual, mature, grown up in the Lord, an adult Christian whose thinking and behavior is becoming of your spiritual age.

In the pages ahead we will take a serious look at this matter. All that glitters is not gold, and gold doesn't always glitter. We are about to look at what true Christian maturity is and is not. We will then look at clear, distinctive earmarks of maturity or the absence thereof. You will be able to determine your level of maturity. You will also learn how to tell the difference between the real thing and the counterfeit.

---

[1] *Webster's New World Dictionary with Student Handbook: Young People's Edition,* s.v. "mature," (Nashville, Tennessee: The World Publishing Company, 1973), 433.

[2] Archibald Thomas Robertson, *Word Pictures in the New Testament,* vol. 4, (Nashville, Tennessee: Broadman Press, 1931), 315.

Chapter 2

Maturity: Its Essence

It is unlikely that any two Christians are at the exact same maturity level. Some are more developed than others. As in physical growth there are stages along the way. As a teenager grows more mature, those around see signs of maturity. Puberty comes on and the body develops. Thought patterns change and he increasingly responds to the realities of life in a more positive and realistic way. Likewise, as a Christian matures spiritually, attitudes and values change for the better, which increases responsible behavior. Here and there lapses will occur, and a Christian may revert to childish ways; but growth to maturity is a trend away from immature thinking and behavior. Paul exemplified and expressed the Christian ideal. *"When I was a child, I spake as a child, I understood as a child, I thought as a child: but when I became a man, I put away childish things,"* **1 Corinthians 13:11**.

Water is wet. It may be salty or fresh, hard or soft, cold or hot. It may be in liquid form, but it may be in the form of steam or ice. Regardless of its many properties and manifestations, water is two molecules of hydrogen in chemical bond with one molecule of oxygen: H_2O. Other ingredients may be added to make the water salty or bitter, but pure water is H_2O.

What is the essence of true *Christian Maturity*? Of what is it composed; not the outward appearance or symptoms, but the nature of it?

A THREE-FOLD ESSENCE

A major theme of 1 Corinthians is spiritual maturity. Early in the letter Paul rebuked the members of the Corinthian Church. He accused them of being *"carnal . . . babes,"* **1 Corinthians 3:1-4**. He was clearly rebuking them for their immaturity. As he later in the book spoke about personal spiritual growth, he identified its essence as *faith, hope* and *charity. "And now abideth faith, hope, charity, these three; but the greatest of these is charity,"* **1 Corinthians 13:13**. No believer can lack any of these and be mature.

Faith

At its core *faith* is belief in God and His Word. It comes through the Word of God. *"So then faith cometh by hearing, and hearing by the Word of God,"* **Romans 10:17**. Faith is not merely believing something strongly or passionately; faith must be based on the Word of God. To believe something apart from a Bible basis is presumption, not faith. (Many confuse faith and presumption.) What God says is true and believing it is faith. That includes God's claims and promises; it also includes acceptance of the Bible's statements about the nature and character of God.

The Word of God (the Bible) is called *"the faith which was once delivered unto the saints,"* **Jude 3**. Notice the use of the definite article which is *the.* In this passage *faith* is used as a noun. This is a reference to the completed Word of God, the Bible. More commonly in the Scriptures *faith* is used as a verb as in 1 Corinthians 13:13. The infinitive Greek verb is pistis meaning "moral conviction." [1] The idea is trust, dependence, believe. Jesus used the word repeatedly. For example, He used the word five times in **John 3:14-18**. *"And as Moses lifted up the serpent in the wilderness, even so must the Son of man be lifted up: That whosoever believeth in him should not perish, but have eternal life. For God so loved the world, that he gave his only begotten Son, that whosoever believeth in him should not perish, but have everlasting life. For God sent not his Son into the world to condemn the world; but that the world through him might be saved. He that believeth on him is not condemned: but he that believeth not* *is condemned already, because he hath not believed in the name of the only begotten Son of God."* True faith is belief, acceptance, confidence, trust in who God is and in what He said. He's right! Every time!

As Christians spiritually mature their faith in God grows. Increasingly their confidence in God and in what He said strengthens. Part of the spiritual maturing process is learning what *the faith* (Bible) teaches and aligning thinking and conduct with it. A young person becomes emotionally mature by adopting a sound system of attitudes, reasoning, and conduct; likewise a believer grows to spiritual maturity by adopting the sound thinking and reasoning of God. In order to do that, he must get into the Word of God to find out what God thinks about divine inspiration, about origins, about who Jesus really is, about business, about morals, about family life, about resolving conflicts, about character, about adversity, about government and every other facet of life. He can never be considered mature until he gives up his own preconceived ideas and begins to think like God thinks on all matters. The more the believer takes God's views, the more mature he is; and once he gets to the point of consciously attempting to take God's position in all matters, he is mature. **2 Corinthians 5:7** calls this kind of *living* walking *"by faith, not by sight."* This is not an occasional act of faith; it is a consistent walk of faith. Yes, he'll continue to fail; but even then he'll take God's position on dealing with his failures.

Since a church is a body of baptized believers covenanted together to keep the ordinances and carry out the great commission, a church will always remain immature until its members grow up to maturity. A church is mature only when it knows what God expects and corporately conducts itself accordingly. On a routine basis! Furthermore, since the pastor is the primary mortal *"example"* in the church, **1 Timothy 4:12**, he will always have an enormous impact on the church for the better or the worse.

Hope

Hope looks ahead and anticipates the hand of God in all things. Though *hope* is akin to *faith*, they are not one and the same. The Greek word for hope is elpis meaning "to anticipate, expectation, confidence" generally with pleasure.[2] Hope follows faith. We can legitimately hope for only that which God has promised. There is no basis for confidence or hope in our own human-engineered plans, but the plans of God shall stand and prevail. It is quite encouraging and comforting to consider that He has many, many plans that relate directly to those who know Him as personal Savior. Hope for believers is all wrapped up in what God has in store for us.

In discussing hope the Apostle Paul said, *"Therefore being justified by faith, we have peace with God through our Lord Jesus Christ: By whom also we have access by faith into this grace wherein we stand, and rejoice in hope of the glory of God. And not only so, but we glory in tribulations also: knowing that tribulation worketh patience; And patience, experience; and experience, hope: And hope maketh not ashamed; because the love of God is shed abroad in our hearts by the Holy Ghost which is given unto us,"* **Romans 5:1-5**. Don't miss the divine logic. He said we *"experience"* the workings of God in our lives. When that happens we see God doing exactly what He promised; watch Him work exactly according to His stated principles. Joshua said it well. *"There failed not ought of any good thing which the LORD had spoken,"* **Joshua 21:45**. Hope is a confidence of what God is going to do based on what He has already done. The more we see anything performed in a certain way, the greater our confidence or hope that it will perform in that same way in future experiences. Thus, experiencing the trustworthiness of God generates a growing hope with every new experience. The confidence of the believer grows with every new level of maturity. That's the reason men like Moses, David, Daniel, and Paul didn't crumble under pressure. They had *"hope,"* confidence in their God, and *"hope maketh not ashamed,"* **Romans 5:5**. I'm not talking about arrogance. I'm talking about a stedfast confidence in God so strong that with it men faced hungry lions, the teeth of Roman power and the scorn of the world. It's a confidence that in spite of the odds and cost, God will prevail: a confidence that *"I'll ultimately prevail with Him though now it costs me everything, including my life."*

We have hope, not only in what God has already done for us, but in what He is going to do for us. *"For we are saved by hope: but hope that is seen is not hope: for what a man seeth, why doth he yet hope for? But if we hope for that we see not, then do we with patience wait for it,"* **Romans 8:24-25**. Note well: we are *"saved"* by hope. We are not saved from sin's penalty by hope; we are saved from despair and spiritual defeat by hope. Paul explained *"And we know that all things work together for good to them that love God, to them who are called according to his purpose,"* **Romans 8:28** and *"If God be for us, who can be against us?"* **Romans 8:31**. Verses 32-39 further confirm God's ability to take care of us under all circumstances.

Not only will God take care of us while we live here on earth, one day He will come again. Jesus personally said it. *"Let not your heart be troubled: ye believe in God, believe also in me. In my Father's house are many mansions: if it were not so, I would have told you. I go to prepare a place for you. And if I go and prepare a place for you, I will come again, and receive you unto myself; that where I am, there ye may be also,"* **John 14:1-3**. The Apostle John said, *"Beloved, now are we the sons of God, and it doth not yet appear what we shall be: but we know that, when he shall appear, we shall be like him; for we shall see him as he is. And every man that hath this hope in him purifieth himself, even as he is pure,"* **1 John 3:2-3**. It is called *"the hope of glory,"* **Colossians 1:27**, and no man can adequately describe the glorious future that lies ahead for believers. *"Blessed be the God and Father of our Lord Jesus Christ, which according to his abundant mercy hath begotten us again unto a lively hope by the resurrection of Jesus Christ from the dead, To an inheritance incorruptible, and undefiled, and that fadeth not away, reserved in heaven for you, Who are kept by the power of God through faith unto salvation ready to be revealed in the last time,"* **1 Peter 1:3-5**. For believers it is *"that blessed hope, and the glorious appearing of the great God and our Saviour Jesus Christ,"* **Titus 2:13**. *"The wicked is driven away in his wickedness: but the righteous hath hope in his death,"* **Proverbs 14:32**.

Hope! What an anchor for the soul! *"Wherein God, willing more abundantly to shew unto the heirs of promise the immutability of his counsel, confirmed it by an oath: That by two immutable things, in which it was impossible for God to lie, we might have a strong consolation, who have fled for refuge to lay hold upon the hope set before us: Which hope we have as an anchor of the soul, both sure and stedfast, and which entereth into that within the veil,"* **Hebrews 6:17-19**. Hope stabilizes life and takes men through the valleys. Confidence in the promises of God keeps men from quitting and is a light in the darkest night.

Hope is a part of the essence which makes up maturity. Without it woven through the fabric of your soul there can be no consistency and lasting strength. Without it the disappointments, hurts and adversities of life are too harsh; but the hope that is in Christ gives strength to *"run with patience the race that is set before us,"* **Hebrews 12:1**.

Charity

Charity is a Bible word for love; not merely emotional or feely love and not even brotherly love. It is deliberate head love, by choice often in spite of rejection and reasons to hate. It does right when it would be easier to do wrong, give up and quit. It does not work on impulse and feelings; it functions on conviction and commitment. This love doesn't do what it feels and emotions demand; it does what is right before God. The Greek words are agapao (verb) and agape (noun). The best definition of it is really a description. *"Charity suffereth long, and is kind; charity envieth not; charity vaunteth not itself, is not puffed up, Doth not behave itself unseemly, seeketh not her own, is not easily provoked, thinketh no evil; Rejoiceth not in iniquity, but rejoiceth in the truth; Beareth all things, believeth all things, hopeth all things, endureth all things. Charity never faileth,"* **1 Corinthians 13:4-8**.

This kind of love is at the heart of Christian maturity. Just as hydrogen is one of the component parts of water and there can be no water without hydrogen, even so true agape love is one of the component parts of spiritual maturity. In fact, of all three components, *"charity"* (always translated from agapao) is *"the greatest,"* **1 Corinthians 13:13**. There can be no spiritual maturity without it. Paul made that very clear. *"Though I speak with the tongues of men and of angels, and have not charity. I am become as sounding brass, or a tinkling cymbal. And though I have the gift of prophecy, and understand all mysteries, and all knowledge and though I have all faith, so that I could remove mountains, and have not charity, I am nothing. And though I bestow all my goods to feed the poor, and though I give my body to be burned, and have not charity, it profiteth me nothing,"* **1 Corinthians 13:1-3**.

There is nothing more important than love, not even faith or hope. What does this say about people who get their feelings hurt and quit, the flighty, the unstable and the inconsistent? It says they're immature. What does it say to those who do what they want to do and what they feel instead of what is right and best? It says they're *babes*. And what about those who get angry and say and do hurtful, ugly things? Childish! And, that is true regardless of how much scripture they can quote, how many profound truths they know, how regular they are to church, how much money they give, how talented they are or what their age is spiritually or physically. Regardless of position, fame or status, without charity no one is spiritually mature. Agape love and maturity are Siamese twins; it is impossible to have one without the other. The lack of either is childishness. Is it any wonder that the Bible says, *"And above all things have fervent charity among yourselves: for charity shall cover the multitude of sins,"* **1 Peter 4:8**? Not *one the same level with*, but *"above!"*

LOOKING AHEAD

The next chapter will deal with spiritual counterfeits. In today's religious world there are many of them. The nature of counterfeiting is to confuse, and Satan is a master at it. As we move forward it is wise for us to recognize at least a few of the more common imitations, some of the disguises that fool many people into mistaking immaturity for maturity.

---

[1] James Strong, *Greek Dictionary of the New Testament,* (Nashville, Tennessee: Abingdon Press, 1958), reference 4102.

[2] Ibid., reference 1680.

Chapter 3

Imitations

OBSERVABLE EVIDENCE

In a rather eye-opening sermon Jesus said, *"Beware of false prophets, which come to you in sheep's clothing, but inwardly they are ravening wolves. Ye shall know them by their fruits. Do men gather grapes of thorns, or figs of thistles? Even so every good tree bringeth forth good fruit; but a corrupt tree bringeth forth evil fruit. A good tree cannot bring forth evil fruit, neither can a corrupt tree bring forth good fruit. Every tree that bringeth not forth good fruit is hewn down, and cast into the fire. Wherefore by their fruits ye shall know them. Not every one that saith unto me, Lord, Lord, shall enter into the kingdom of heaven; but he that doeth the will of my Father which is in heaven. Many will say to me in that day, Lord, Lord, have we not prophesied in thy name? and in thy name have cast out devils? and in thy name done many wonderful works? And then will I profess unto them, I never knew you: depart from me, ye that work iniquity,"* **Matthew 7:15-23**. Obviously everything is not what it appears to be. Fool's gold looks real, but it's not; and some professing Christians look mature, but they are not.

THE POSSIBLIITY OF IMITATIONS

Faith, hope and charity! They can be imitated.

In the natural world there are masters of imitation and camouflage. Things are not always what they appear to be. What appears to be a rock in a coral reef may be an archer fish. Rabbits rarely recognize the snares that hang them. Counterfeiting is an old and widespread practice. Counterfeits can easily be mistaken for the real thing.

Many are mistaken about what constitutes Christian maturity. Often people who are extremely childish and immature are viewed as spiritual giants. Here is a short list of mistaken ideas.

Piousness

There are those who act very pious, devout, holy and *saintly*. They *appear to be* extremely mature in the Lord. They have *that look* about them. It has been said of some people that *they are so heavenly minded that they are of no earthly good.* Maturity is not merely in a look; it always involves ability and performance. Empty platitudes matter little. James asked, *"What doth it profit, my brethren, though a man say he hath faith, and have not works,"* **James 2:14**? It's not enough to talk about and pretend honesty; you need to practice honesty, and dependability, and helping others, and selflessness, and soul-winning and mentoring. Show your maturity by your routine performance of vintage Christianity; empty words and looks mean nothing. The Pharisees and Sadducees of the Bible were quite pious, but they were hypocrites of the highest sort.

Piety is good providing it is real, but it cannot be equated with maturity. Piety may come with maturity, but a mature Christian may not seem pious at all.

Chest Beating

Mature Christians do not brag about it, and they will not find it necessary to tell you they are. The Bible says, *"Let another man praise thee, and not thine own mouth; a stranger, and not thine own lips,"* **Proverbs 27:2**. As we will see later in this book, pride is not of God. Humility, not self-exaltation is a mark of a mature Christian. There are lots of ways to exalt self, both overtly and covertly. The mouths of some Christians are full of *I, me* and *what I have done.* Others are more subtle. They name-drop, tell how others brag on them and say how great others say they are, highlight how they've helped others and what they've done for others, speak of where they've been and what they've done and always have a bigger and better story or opinion. Somehow they are always the center of most of their stories. Ironically, those who make a point of *hating glory hogs and other forms of* self-exaltation are often chiefs in that practice. It has been well said that *neither those who are full of pride nor those who are genuinely humble seem to know it.*

Animated Church Behavior

Some people are really good at *putting on* a *church show.* They can turn on the passion and emotions at just the right time: the tears, the *amens* and *hallelujahs*, the hands in the air, the theatrics in a song or sermon, the trips to *the altar.* And people buy it; they think these are the pillars in the church.

If these behaviors are real and from the heart, they are good; but if they are *for show* and to gain *the praise of men,* **Matthew 6:1-8**, then they are mockery to God. Only God knows the heart and the true motives behind behavior. Beware lest you become a judge of motives, but never assume animated church behavior is the same as Christian maturity. There are clear-cut marks of Christian maturity, but animated church behavior is not one of them.

Prolific Use of Scriptures

Often bystanders equate prolific use of Scriptures (especially in preachers) to be a sign of great depth and maturity. It is not. The Devil is a master at quoting Scriptures and the Pharisees were very good at it, but they weren't even saved. The verses a Christian can quote are not nearly as important as those he lives. Prolific use of Scriptures correctly used by godly people is a wonderful habit, and it certainly does not say one is immature; but neither is it positive proof that he is mature.

Faithfulness to Church

Who could argue with faithfulness to church? God expects it of His people, *"And let us consider one another to provoke unto love and to good works: Not forsaking the assembling of ourselves together, as the manner of some is; but exhorting one another: and so much the more, as ye see the day approaching,"* **Hebrews 10:24-25**. Mature people will be faithful to attend and support the church of God, yet many immature believers go to church like clockwork. Many of them are cold, heartless and carnal. Faithfulness to church and Christian maturity are not one and the same.

Great Involvement in Church Activities

Biblical Martha, **Luke 10:38-42**, is a classic example of a believer who is busy, but immature. The records are full of lost people who were and are deeply involved in church activities. It's good to be busy in the work of God through His church, but just being busy and involved in church does not prove a thing about Christian maturity. Some of the most childish, immature Christians you will ever meet are head-over-heels in church work. Sometimes they are in charge and can be a serious source of hindrance and offence to the work of the Lord.

Great Involvement in Good Social Projects

The same can be said about good community and social projects. Both lost and saved people can get *caught up* in benevolent community work, especially if it has a *holy* feel to it. There seems to be something infectious about *busyness.*

Most Christians ought to be more involved than they are in helping others both inside and outside the church. Deep involvement may be a sign of sincerity and compassion. It is not a sign of faith, hope and charity; and that's what maturity is.

The Declaration of Others

No person is mature because others say he is. Occasionally the opinions of others are right about one's maturity level; but if a person is not truly a person of faith, hope and charity, then he is not mature regardless of what people say. Sometimes people attain a reputation that is bigger than reality and not in sync with it. Most bystanders are not up close and personal enough to see reality. Never assume a person is spiritually mature because people say he is.

Old Spiritual Age

How nice it would be if the spiritual ages of believers actually matched their maturity levels! Such is not often the case. As we've already seen in this book, many believers are still *babes* even after they've had plenty of time to mature. Do not imagine that because a person has been saved a long time he has grown up in the Lord. Praise God for *"them that are of full age, even those who by reason of use have their senses exercised to discern both good and evil,"* **Hebrews 5:14**. A maturity level that matches the spiritual age is not the case with every believer.

GO FOR THE TREASURE, NOT THE WRAPPING PAPER

It's easy to be distracted. Posturing is quite effective. When many animals feel threatened or wish to fight, they make themselves look as big and tough as possible. The hair goes up, the teeth show and the bluffing begins. Don't be deceived or taken-in by diversions. Jesus said, *"Labour not for the meat which perisheth, but for that meat which endureth unto everlasting life, which the Son of man shall give unto you: for him hath God the Father sealed,"* **John 6:27**. Don't be taken-in by counterfeits or seek after them. Keep your eye on the real thing: faith, hope and charity. Go for that of eternal value; don't settle for less.

Christian maturity is precious, especially in the sight of God. The third chapter of 2 Peter is primarily addressed to Christian women, but what Peter said in verse 4 is good advice for all of us. *"But let it be the hidden man of the heart, in that which is not corruptible, even the ornament of a meek and quiet spirit, which is in the sight of God of great price,"* **1 Peter 3:4**.

GLANCING AHEAD

There are ways to tell domestic cattle from horses or pigs. There are even ways to tell these cattle from similar wild animals such as moose, elk or water buffalo. It's not too difficult to tell a Hereford from a Holstein or Brahma. Likewise there are definitive ways to identify mature Christians.

In the chapters ahead we will turn our attention to positive, definitive earmarks of Christian maturity. We are about to see how to tell real, mature Christians from those who are not.

THE CHARACTERISTICS OF MATURITY

Chapter 4

Fundamental Honesty

OBSERVABLE EVIDENCE

Christian maturity is composed of faith, hope and charity; but as good as those qualities are, men cannot see them. People can see only what faith, hope and charity produce; the evidence of their presence. Only God looks directly on the heart; everybody else looks on *"the outward appearance,"* **1 Samuel 16:7**.

Faith, hope and charity produce observable effects as surely as the sun produces light and heat. These effects are specific and concrete earmarks of maturity. A believer may not be fully mature in every way, but it is possible to be mature in one area and yet lack maturity in another. There are characteristics in a believer that indicate he is growing up and maturing. The absence of these characteristics speaks of spiritual immaturity in a Christian.

We will now turn our attention to characteristics which constitute clear evidence of Christian maturity.

WHAT FUNDAMENTAL HONESTY IS

In short *fundamental honesty* is truth in word and deed. It is consistency, one set of weights and measures, a harmonic belief system, practices in agreement with ideological positions and truth regardless of the consequences. An honest person is unbiased, impartial and unprejudiced. He is candid, straight, matter of fact and pulls no punches. Honesty is committed to truth.

An honest person is objective. He is a person who sees, thinks and acts only upon the basis of truth and reality. He neither inflates nor deflates a picture and is not biased or influenced by any person or factor. Nothing is assumed; he requires people who communicate with him to deal in facts and evidence, not rumors and circumstance. An honest and objective person does not draw conclusions and make decisions apart from well-researched, intelligent, and factual considerations.

Fundamental honesty is God's way. He *"cannot lie,"* **Titus 1:2**. There is no inconsistency in Him; *"no variableness, neither shadow of turning,"* **James 1:17**. *"God is no respecter of persons,"* **Acts 10:34**. We trust God because He is totally impartial. *"The wisdom that is from above is first pure, then peaceable, gentle, and easy to be intreated, full of mercy and good fruits, without partiality, and without hypocrisy,"* **James 3:17**. What a declaration of fundamental honesty! This is *"from above;"* it is God's way: *"pure"* (holy), *"gentle"* (fair and reasonable), *"without partiality"* (no variance), *"without hypocrisy"* (not hypocritical, but *unfeigned*). [1] God wants every child of His *"to be conformed to the image of his Son,"* **Romans 8:29**. We're to be like Him, and that demands fundamental honesty. *"I charge thee before God, and the Lord Jesus Christ, and the elect angels, that thou observe these things without preferring one before another, doing nothing by partiality,"* **1 Timothy 5:21**. *"Without preferring one before another"* literally means *without prejudgment* and *"doing nothing by partiality"* forbids decisions or actions based on personal inclinations.[2]

At this point it would be easy to step forward and say, *That's me. I'm always impartial, always objective in my decisions and judgment calls. In me there is nothing but fundamental honesty.* It is unlikely that most of us are objective about our own selves, let alone in our opinions and dealings in life. It's pretty hard to be objective about whether or not we are objective; but one thing is certain: if we are not truly objective about ourselves, we'll never be very objective in our thinking and dealings with others.

FACTORS THAT HINDER FUNDAMENTAL HONESTY

Satan is the author of confusion. He constantly inserts diversions and mitigating factors to confuse the facts and cloud issues. He hates the truth. Jesus said Satan is *"a liar, and the father of it,"* **John 8:44**. Believer, do not be surprised when Satan moves in your heart to make you fundamentally dishonest. He has many tried and proven ways.

Respect of Persons

How many times have you heard that *blood is thicker than water?* The message is quite clear; family obligations and connections are more important than those made between unrelated people such as friends. In his last novel which he titled *The Family,* Mario Puzo said, "Blood is thicker than holy water." [3] Puzo put into words what most of us know (and practice): if there's a conflict between what is right (what is taught in the Word of God) and your family, stick with your family. Oh yes, Christians will talk with sweaty passion about truth and about standing without wavering on *thus saith the Lord*; but when it comes to a showdown between *my kid and your kid, let's leave the Bible out of this.* All that Bible stuff about sex outside of marriage, abortions, drug abuse, homosexuality, divorce, paying your debts and other such things is good; *but this is my son, my daughter.*

Remember the words of **1 Timothy 5:21**. *"I charge thee before God, and the Lord Jesus Christ, and the elect angels, that thou observe these things without preferring one before another, doing nothing by partiality."* It is a sad commentary on the Christian world that friends, persons we like and especially our families almost always get preferential treatment than others. When there is a problem, suspicion, conflict or show-down, we automatically assume they are right and the other party is wrong; most of the time we do not even bother to consider the facts or evidence. Even when the facts are conclusive, too often we are double-minded. For example, if another person's child gets into moral trouble, marriage trouble or drugs, we come down hard and very critical. If it's our own child, we expect understanding, compassion and clemency. Clearly many of us have one standard for our own, but another standard for others, especially for those we don't like.

It is fundamentally dishonest for anyone, especially a Christian, to falsify anything for any reason. Yet, it is a common practice in the Christian community. Sometimes old, pious church members skew judgments because of people: family members, business partners, old buddies, people they like. And they think they are mature! Maturity is honest. It calls a spade a spade. It is not into prejudice; it doesn't look at people in terms of race, color, riches, friendships or family. Maturity knows that only *"the truth shall make you free,"* **John 8:32**. It does not pervert judgment. Maturity is not ugly about it, but it focuses on truth and reality regardless of the personalities involved.

Self-Interests

The flesh is a great enemy to all of us. We live in a fleshly body and it has ravenous appetites of a great variety. The flesh is always looking out for itself *"to fulfil the lusts thereof,"* **Romans 13:14**. The flesh is extremely selfish. The Apostle Paul spoke for all Christians when he said, *"I am carnal, sold under sin. For that which I do I allow not: for what I would, that do I not; but what I hate, that do I. If then I do that which I would not, I consent unto the law that it is good. Now then it is no more I that do it, but sin that dwelleth in me. For I know that in me (that is, in my flesh,) dwelleth no good thing: for to will is present with me; but how to perform that which is good I find not. For the good that I would I do not: but the evil which I would not, that I do. Now if I do that I would not, it is no more I that do it, but sin that dwelleth in me. I find then a law, that, when I would do good, evil is present with me,"* **Romans 7:14-21**.

In the interest of itself the flesh has no problem with being dishonest. To get its way and insure its comfort it will embellish and doctor a story, blame (even an innocent person), duck-out on responsibility, hide when it ought to be standing and lie in lots of other ways. Self-interests blind and distort. Actions taken in self-interest will invariably be biased and out of touch with reality and righteousness. Here is a biblical description of men who are *"lovers of their own selves."* You will find it in **2 Timothy 3:2-7**. *"For men shall be lovers of their own selves, covetous, boasters, proud, blasphemers, disobedient to parents, unthankful, unholy, Without natural affection, trucebreakers, false accusers, incontinent, fierce, despisers of those that are good, Traitors, heady, highminded, lovers of pleasures more than lovers of God; Having a form of godliness, but denying the power thereof: from such turn away. For of this sort are they which creep into houses, and lead captive silly women laden with sins, led away with divers lusts, Ever learning, and never able to come to the knowledge of the truth."*

Christian maturity is renouncing *"the hidden things of dishonesty, not walking in craftiness, nor handling the word of God deceitfully; but by manifestation of the truth commending ourselves to every man's conscience in the sight of God,"* **2 Corinthians 4:2**. It is learning to speak and live the truth in all honesty both with self and others. Maturity does not allow self to distort truth and reality.

Preconceived Notions

My mind is already made up; don't confuse me with the facts is not merely a cute one-liner. It is really easy to jump to premature conclusions. We get bits and pieces of a story and here we go making up our mind when the verdict is still out (especially when it's juicy and related to someone or some issue where we already have strong opinions). *I already know what I believe on this Bible issue; nobody's going to change my mind.* So, we don't even listen. And we think we're mature! We scorn at the closed-minded scientific community many of which have already concluded that there is no God. They approach everything from the humanistic worldview that all knowledge comes from man. They have precluded that everything can be naturally explained. They will not even consider the possibility of divine revelation. We then turn around and close our minds on issue after issue. In fact, jumping to conclusions can become a way of life for Christians.

Jesus said, *"In the mouth of two or three witnesses every word may be established,"* **Matthew 18:16**. The Christian who acts upon inadequate research and evidence is acting with extreme immaturity. King Solomon said, *"He that answereth a matter before he heareth it, it is folly and shame unto him,"* **Proverbs 18:13**. Nicodemus asked his peers in Jewish leadership, *"Doth our law judge any man, before it hear him, and know what he doeth?"* **John 7:51**. God forbid that any believer would ever be so immature as to allow his preconceived notions to destroy his ability to see and act on things in truth and reality! Maturity is acting toward the matters of life as they are in truth and reality. Mature people do not allow preconceived notions to distort their thinking.

Unbridled Passions

Anger, fear, hatred, impatience, pride and other such fleshly weaknesses destroy our ability to be objective. It is amazing how much different a person can think and act when he is angry or afraid. These high emotions are like drugs to the spirit. They loosen the tongue, blur the vision and dull the hearing. They addle the senses of justice and excite the senses of violence, cruelty and dominance. Multitudes have made fools out of themselves in a *fit of rage* or passion. Usually to their later regret and deep sorrow! Cussing fits, fist fights and even murder and other violence!

It becomes virtually impossible to think and act objectively while mad or deeply fearful. Solomon said, *"He that is hasty of spirit exalteth folly,"* **Proverbs 14:29**. No man who forms opinions, makes decisions or acts in anger or fear can be considered mature. Paul said those who would be mature in the Lord must put away *"all bitterness, and wrath, and anger, and clamour, and evil speaking,"* along with all *"malice,"* **Ephesians 4:31**.

Unbridled passions speak of immaturity, even in Christians who can quote lots of Scripture, who can put on an impressive show in church and who are generally very pious. A mature Christian is one whose passions are under control. James pointed out that a person's control of his tongue is a good indication of his overall control of self or the lack thereof. He said, *"For in many things we offend all. If any man offend not in word, the same is a perfect man, and able also to bridle the whole body,"* **James 3:2**.

The Distortion of Those Involved in a Matter

Perhaps one of the most successful enemies of fundamental honesty is the deliberate distortion of those involved in a matter. It seems that everybody has *an axe to grind.* Whether to win a theological argument, to hide their sins and guilt, to make themselves look better, to win a fight or to foster some other vested interest, people will deliberately distort and shade the truth.

Half-truths, hidden evidence, distorted verbal pictures, emphasis on the minors of the case and fingers pointed in judgment are just some of the tactics people (even those close to us) use to distort our spiritual vision, judgment and activity. The likelihood is very great that every one of us has been guilty of using these very tactics to gain support to our side. Paul spoke of the unrighteous ways of humans. *"Their throat is an open sepulchre; with their tongues they have used deceit; the poison of asps is under their lips,"* **Romans 3:13**. That's not a very pretty picture, but it is the truth about how we are. The sad part is that other people are taken in by these tactics, often to the extent that they simply will not see and act objectively. Solomon said, *"The folly of fools is deceit,"* **Proverbs 14:8**; yet a great many of our decisions and actions are based on these smokescreens: from our children, from our friends, from the news media and even from preachers.

Christian growth is increasing in our ability to deal with distortions and smokescreens.

STAYING WITH THE TRUTH

As Christians grow up they increasingly become people of honesty: in words, in deeds, in overall consistency. They become truly objective people who are not easily *taken in* by anything. They are not perfect and can still be vulnerable, but they are no longer *"children, tossed to and fro, and carried about with every wind of doctrine, by the sleight of men, and cunning craftiness, whereby they lie in wait to deceive;"* but they speak *"the truth in love"* and *"grow up into him in all things, which is the head, even Christ,"* **Ephesians 4:14-15**. They do not make matters more or less than they are. They look beyond the personalities, smokescreens, passions, self-interests and other influences that tend to interfere with fundamental honesty.

Whether the matter involves friend or foe, they apply Bible principles and reach biblical conclusions. They do not consider what's best for self in the matter; they consider what is right. They do not fly into rages of emotion and make decisions on whims; instead they decide deliberately and rationally according to those principles of justice and righteousness which they find in the Bible. Solomon put it this way: *"The heart of the righteous studieth to answer,"* **Proverbs 15:28**. David said, *"The mouth of the righteous speaketh wisdom, and his tongue talketh of judgment,"* **Psalm 37:30**.

We're talking about real, tangible evidence of Christian maturity, the kind of behavior produced by faith, hope and charity. We're looking at a person who acts on biblical principles, upon truth and reality; and one who refuses to act otherwise. We're talking about a life of action, not reaction, about one who has the patience and restraint of spirit to do his homework, get the facts and make sound judgments and actions based on truth and reality in light of God's Word. This is that fruit of the spirit called *"temperance"* (Holy Spirit control), **Galatians 5:23**. This is that condition of which James spoke, *"But let patience have her perfect work, that ye may be perfect and entire, wanting nothing,"* **James 1:4**. We're looking at Christian maturity. This kind of consistent objectivity says a man has it, while its absence cries immaturity. This is tangible evidence.

THERE IS MORE

Christian maturity manifests itself in more than one way. Fundamental honesty is an unmistakable sign or earmark, but there are other distinctive earmarks. The next chapter will deal with *humility*. Talk about a revealing sign. Humility speaks volumes for those who have it, but it also speaks volumes for those who do not have it.

---

1 A.T. Robertson, *Word Pictures in the New Testament,* vol. 6, (Nashville, Tennessee: Broadman Press, 1933), 47.

2 Robertson, vol. 4, 589.

3 *Wikipedia,* (en.wikipedia.org/wiki/Blood_is_thicker_than_water).

Chapter 5

Humility

A case is rarely built on one piece of evidence; usually many pieces of evidence combine to make an irrefutable case. Fundamental honesty is evidence, a definitive earmark of Christian maturity; but there is more. There are other earmarks. One of them is humility.

UNDERSTANDING TRUE HUMILITY

Many ancient kings made sure that two doors entering their palaces had clearances so low that all who entered must bow. Bowing and kneeling are widely recognized as acts of submission. Even though submission wasn't always genuine and from the heart, those kings wanted a show of humility from those who approached them.

Humility: submission, meekness, humbleness, unpretentious, respect, on bended knee. True humility embodies lowliness or humbleness of mind as well as appropriate actions. Humility recognizes one's own weaknesses and faults. It is recognition that all anyone has or is comes through the goodness and grace of God. The Bible makes a rather piercing point. *"For who maketh thee to differ from another? and what hast thou that thou didst not receive? now if thou didst receive it, why dost thou glory, as if thou hadst not received it?"*

1 Corinthians 4:7. We all came here with nothing, and we'll all leave here with nothing. Recognition of that reality humbles honest men. It takes away the brashness, superiority, posturing and chest-beating that is so common among men. It puts a damper on seeking the limelight and the praise of men.

As great as Moses was when his father-in-law came to him after the Israeli exodus from Egypt, *"Moses went out to meet his father in law, and did obeisance,"* **Exodus 18:7**. This word *"obeisance"* is from the Hebrew word <u>shachah</u> meaning *prostrate or bow down one's self.* Sometimes people stooped; they often fell face-down on the ground in their respect and deference to another.[1] A man of Moses' status could have ignored or exercised dominance and superiority over Jethro; however, he humbled himself before the father of his wife. It is noteworthy that the Bible says, *"Now the man Moses was very meek, above all the men which were upon the face of the earth,"* **Numbers 12:3**. Moses voluntarily submitted (humbled himself) to another person. Moses exemplifies true humility (and great maturity).

Humility obviously has to do with one's appraisal of self. It is closely related to fundamental honesty but goes a step farther; humility applies fundamental honesty to self. It recognizes one's own accomplishments and position, but it chooses not to flaunt them. It is honest enough to not deflate who and where one is in life; but it does not use status and accomplishments to inflate, glorify, to exalt self or to subdue others. One can be mighty and still be humble.

THAT OLD RASCAL CALLED SELF

We all know who self is. He's that part of us that always wants his way. Self gives us grief. It says and does what it shouldn't, is seldom considerate of others and is always looking out for its own interests. Self is egotistical, loves to be petted and glories in the limelight. *Mine is better than yours. My daddy can whip your daddy. I know something you don't know. I have something you don't have. Look at my degrees, my trophies, what I've done and where I've been. I shook hands with the president. My great uncle was a U. S. Congressman.* When I was in high school, the family of one of my classmates bought a Ford Edsel. For the next several days we were bombarded with *"We got an Edsel."*

Jesus identified self with the flesh and said, *"The flesh is weak,"* **Matthew 26:41**. Oh yes, it is truly *weak* in character and goodness, but is extremely strong in its resistance to God and His righteousness. The Apostle Peter warned, *"Dearly beloved, I beseech you as strangers and pilgrims, abstain from fleshly lusts, which war against the soul,"* **1 Peter 2:11**. The Apostle John also warned, *"Love not the world, neither the things that are in the world. If any man love the world, the love of the Father is not in him. For all that is in the world, the lust of the flesh, and the lust of the eyes, and the pride of life, is not of the Father, but is of the world. And the world passeth away, and the lust thereof,"* **1 John 2:15-17**.

Self will take away your humility. Self wants to be exalted and inflated. It wants to dominate, not be dominated. It wants the credit, the limelight, the praise, the glory.

THE BIBLE CALLS SELF-EXALTATION PRIDE

Pride! An enemy royal! The great prophet Ezekiel provides insight into the once-beautiful angel Lucifer. *"Thou art the anointed cherub that covereth; and I have set thee so: thou wast upon the holy mountain of God; thou hast walked up and down in the midst of the stones of fire. Thou wast perfect in thy ways from the day that thou wast created, till iniquity was found in thee,"* **Ezekiel 28:14-15**. The *iniquity*? Pride! Self exaltation! No submission! *My way and what I want, my way or the highway. I will rule.* Another great prophet named Isaiah enunciated the matter. *"How art thou fallen from heaven, O Lucifer, son of the morning! how art thou cut down to the ground, which didst weaken the nations! For thou hast said in thine heart, I will ascend into heaven, I will exalt my throne above the stars of God: I will sit also upon the mount of the congregation, in the sides of* *the north: I will ascend above the heights of the clouds; I will be like the most High,"* **Isaiah 14:12-14**.

The English word *pride* comes from the Greek word tuphoo. The root of that word means "to make a smoke, i.e. slowly consume without flame." [2] The idea is "to inflate with self-conceit: - high-minded, be lifted up with pride, be proud." [3] Webster defines proud as "thinking too highly of oneself; conceited; vain or haughty; arrogant." [4]

The Bible says, *"Pride goeth before destruction, and an haughty spirit before a fall,"* **Proverbs 16:18**. The Hebrew word for pride is gaon meaning "arrogancy, excellency (-lent), majesty, pomp, pride, proud, swelling." [5] When facing a confrontation, most animals inflate themselves. The ears flare or lay back, the hair stands up, the back arches. The animals have intimidation and domination on their minds. There's a sizeable streak of that spirit in humans and some let it *hang out.* They inflate themselves and seek to subdue and dominate others in both normal and confrontational situations. *I'm bigger, stronger, better, richer, smarter, prettier, badder!* Pride; it's the way of the world. Jesus said it, *"Ye know that the princes of the Gentiles exercise dominion over them, and they that are great exercise authority upon them,"* **Matthew 20:25**. He went on to say that this is not the way of God and Christian maturity and greatness. *"But it shall not be so among you: but whosoever will be great among you, let him be your minister; And whosoever will be chief among you, let him be your servant: Even as the Son of man came not to be ministered unto, but to minister, and to give his life a ransom for many,"* **Matthew 20:26-28**. He was talking humility. It's the way of honesty about self and the situation. He was teaching voluntary submission and service; saying that final credit and praise should be given only to God which is where they belong.

Pride is man's worst enemy: *I'm secure. Nobody can touch me. I can whip him. Nobody will ever find out. I'm the best."* Jesus told about a proud farmer who had a great crop. The farmer said, *"This will I do: I will pull down my barns, and build greater; and there will I bestow all my fruits and my goods. And I will say to my soul, Soul, thou hast much goods laid up for many years; take thine ease, eat, drink, and be merry,"* **Luke 12:18-19**. A picture of pride, arrogance and self-sufficiency! A picture of most people! *"But God said unto him, Thou fool, this night thy soul shall be required of thee: then whose shall those things be, which thou hast provided?"* **Luke 12:20**. Pride, self-will, dishonesty about self and the reality of the overall picture is the perfect formula for disaster! *"Every one that is proud in heart is an abomination to the LORD: though hand join in hand, he shall not be unpunished,"* **Proverbs 16:5**. *"I will cause the arrogancy of the proud to cease,"* **Isaiah 13:11**. Pride really does go *"before destruction, and an haughty spirit before a fall,"* **Proverbs 16:18**.

THE STABILIZING POWER OF HUMILITY

Jesus said, *"Ye shall know the truth, and the truth shall make you free,"* **John 8:32**. The truth is honest: about self, about others, about the situation. Honesty looks at things from God's viewpoint and submits to the fact that this is God's world. An honest man is a humble man. He doesn't need to dominate, be the big boss or have the praise of other people. He is content and secure in his position in Christ. Why should he beat his own chest? He knows the way to greatness is in submission and service.

Before he was saved, Paul (then Saul of Tarsus) was an extremely proud and domineering man. Oh, what a pedigree he had! Listen to his confession. *"If any other man thinketh that he hath whereof he might trust in the flesh, I more: Circumcised the eighth day, of the stock of Israel, of the tribe of Benjamin, an Hebrew of the Hebrews; as touching the law, a Pharisee; Concerning zeal, persecuting the church; touching the righteousness which is in the law, blameless,"* **Philippians 3:4-6**. This man met Christ and began to grow up or mature in the Lord. As he matured he *"put away childish things,"* **1 Corinthians 13:11**. We know that one thing he put away was pride. *"What things were gain to me, those I counted loss for Christ,"* **Philippians 3:7**. He still had that grand pedigree, but it paled in light of what he found in Christ. Read his story. After he met Christ he no longer went forth flexing his academic muscle or his native heritage. He no longer went forth to subdue and conquer men with raw power and force as he had done before. He went as a humble servant of God seeking to win men. A radical change occurred. He came to Christ and grew up to maturity *"serving the LORD with all humility of mind,"* **Acts 20:19**. Even in a jail cell he could say, *"I have learned, in whatsoever state I am, therewith to be content,"* **Philippians 4:11**. Humility does that to men. Peter said, *"Ye younger, submit yourselves unto the elder. Yea, all of you be subject one to another, and be clothed with humility: for God resisteth the proud, and giveth grace to the humble,"* **1 Peter 5:5**.

As people mature in the Lord they become more and more humble; not more proud, conceited and domineering. It has been well said that neither the proud nor the humble know they are. Bystanders know. Neither condition is difficult to recognize. It is noteworthy that Peter continued his discussion about humility with these words, *"Humble yourselves therefore under the mighty hand of God, that he may exalt you in due time,"* **1 Peter 5:6**. Notice that *humble* is used in the verb form and is reflexive. The subject is *you*: *"You humble yourselves."* The initiative is on *you*, not God. He is more than capable of humbling us, but He wants us to humble ourselves. He expects us to deal with the pride, conceit and selfishness in our lives. People who are proud and arrogant cannot blame their condition on God. He has put the power to address pride and become humble in our hands. As we do, we grow and become increasingly mature and Christ-like. *"He humbled himself,"* **Philippians 2:8.** He who had the power to subdue all powers deliberately and voluntarily subjected Himself, even to the cross. Humility is not too much for Him to ask of us.

All glory belongs to God. Yes, *"all."* No person is to seek self and self glory. God gave us our existence and made us all we are. Thus, He alone deserves the glory. Listen to Paul say this, *"But God hath chosen the foolish things of the world to confound the wise; and God hath chosen the weak things of the world to confound the things which are mighty; And base things of the world, and things which are despised, hath God chosen, yea, and things which are not, to bring to nought things that are:*

That no flesh should glory in his presence. But of him are ye in Christ Jesus, who of God is made unto us wisdom, and righteousness, and sanctification, and redemption: That, according as it is written, He that glorieth, let him glory in the Lord," **1 Corinthians 1:27-31**. A grasp of that great truth will take the pride right out of a person and replace it with humble gratitude to God. There are no grounds for self-exaltation. Why should any preacher gloat over a great sermon or church? Why should any singer have a *"big head"* over a great voice? God gave the ability to make money and all other abilities and talents. There are no *"Big I's"* among mature Christians.

Mature people are humble. They want God to get the credit and praise for all things including what He has used them to do. They want Him in the limelight. They are full of gratitude for what God has done, and do not have their attention on *self*. They rejoice at His work whether it is through them or others. Jealousy is not a part of their thinking.

Genuine humility is an unmistakable sign of Christian maturity and a lack of it is a sure sign of immaturity. (I say *genuine humility* because people have the capacity to pretend or fake humility. You will find a discussion of this cheap trait in **Colossians 3:18-23**.) The prodigal son exemplifies growth, the transition from pride to humility; immaturity to maturity. **Luke 15:11-21**. At the beginning of the story this son was proud, arrogant, demanding and out for self. At the end of the story he saw himself as a humble and undeserving servant. As people grow up in the Lord, this is the transition that invariably takes place. A saved person may be old, talented, smart in the Bible and as faithful as the tides and still be a spiritual babe; but when humility becomes a part of his being, there is maturity.

THERE ARE OTHER EARMARKS OF MATURITY

Truly mature people are not one-dimensional (mature in one area but babes in another). Their maturity manifests itself on many fronts. There are many earmarks. The next chapter of this book deals with personal discipline. We will explore the area of Holy Spirit control. You may be surprised at how personal discipline and Holy Spirit control work hand-in-hand with each other.

---

[1] James Strong, *Hebrew and Chaldee Dictionary,* (Nashville, Tennessee: Abingdon Press, 1958), reference 7812.

[2] James Strong, *Greek Dictionary of the New Testament,* (Nashville, Tennessee: Abingdon Press, 1958), reference 5188.

[3] Ibid., reference 5187.

[4] *Webster's New World Dictionary with Student Handbook: Young People's Edition,* s.v. "proud," (Nashville, Tennessee: The World Publishing Company, 1973), 556.

[5] *Hebrew and Chaldee Dictionary,* reference 1347.

Chapter 6

Personal Discipline

When I was an early teenage lad, my family lived in the big East Texas piney woods outside of Lufkin. My dad hired loggers who harvested several huge pine trees off his property, some in front of our house. They took the big logs, but left the tops and ends of limbs which quickly turned brown. These pine-tops were tender boxes because they were dead, drying and full of resin. One spark could turn them almost instantly into a blazing inferno. One day a close neighbor and pal of mine got hold of a cigarette. Boys love climbing into a hidden place, especially when they are up to no good. That afternoon he and I climbed into one of those pine-tops; we were excited to smoke our first cigarette. We were oblivious to the fact that my rather fiery-tempered dad was sitting on the front porch of our house less than 100 yards away (or to the long-term impacts of tobacco on one's body). Dad saw the smoke rising from our cozy tender-box. What happened next was not very pleasant. When dad finished with me, I was resolved never to smoke again. I am happy to say that I have kept that resolution.

A CHILDHOOD CHARACTERISTIC

We expect children to be undisciplined; it's a childhood characteristic. *"Foolishness is bound in the heart of a child,"* **Proverbs**

22:15. They leave their clothes right where they take them off, usually on the floor. They are not into baths and cleanliness. A sleeve is better than a napkin, the same dirty clothes will work for many days and a dip in the pool is as a good as a shower with soap. Often the results are odors, rashes and frustrated mothers. When teeth are neglected the results can be rather costly cavities. Look at the average teenager's bedroom. Order and cleanliness are rare. They like sweets and treats over nutrition. Vegetables! Anathema! *Give me pizza, ice cream and candy!* They are not into dangers, restraints or consequences, especially long-term consequences. Children have a difficult time keeping their days and nights from getting mixed up, putting their toys in the toy box and thinking much about the needs of others. Most playground scenes are kids playing together, not with each other. There is a vast difference.

Discipline, self-control, responsibility and such things simply have not yet reached their radars. They're just kids, *foot-lose and fancy-free.* It's mostly about self and *what I want.* When their way does not prevail it is not unlikely for a tantrum to erupt. Most parents know something about an *attitude.*

GROWING UP

As children grow up we expect these traits to go away. They are to learn self-control and how to discipline or police themselves: to control their appetites and temper, to make good food and friend choices, to respect others and clean up their own messes. Somehow between birth and adulthood, a person who would succeed in life must learn to take care of his self. He will not always have a mother there to clean up his body and room, wash his dirty clothes, get him out of bed on time, cook his meals, or teach him how to interface with others or see that he meets his responsibilities. There will not always be a dad there to pay the rent and utilities, buy the groceries, provide a car, to give attention to medical needs and point out what is right and wrong. Growing up is a steady progression in self-discipline.

A SAD REALITY

A sad and growing characteristic of modern society is its lack of discipline. Children are growing up without the basic skills needed to survive (personally and as a society). Many physically mature adults have little if any sense of personal discipline, responsibility, loyalty or duty. A solid work ethic is rare and it is difficult to find a Good Samaritan who is genuinely concerned about the rights or welfare of others. Too many physically mature people are frightfully undisciplined and selfish. Multitudes are given to unrestrained appetites: alcohol, food, sex, material things, popularity, entertainment and other pleasures.

Why? At least one of the major contributors to this wave of *little restraint* in which we find our world is lack of godly parenting. From birth, children are mostly unrestrained. They never have or learn firm boundaries. Spanking or corporal punish is frowned on by society. Little is required of children: no garbage or lawn duties, few restraints on video games or cell phones, little effort by parents to know where their children are or what kind of friends they have, very little supervision of the websites they visit and hardly a thought to instill the great Christian virtues that help people police their selves. Rather than learn discipline, masses of modern children are learning self-indulgence.

It is not uncommon for parents and grandparents to think the rebellious, undisciplined ways of their child are *"so cute."* The consequences of such behavior are not immediately apparent. Solomon observed, *"Because sentence against an evil work is not executed speedily, therefore the heart of the sons of men is fully set on them to do evil,"* **Ecclesiastes 8:11**. As an undisciplined person grows older, those ways are not nearly so *cute.* Oh the rude awakening and anguish that often comes to parents when the teenage years arrive: *My child is on drugs, my daughter is pregnant,* whispers about an abortion, that call in the night from the police, Junior robbed a convenience store and is in a gang, *my precious child was in the car when it rounded the curve at a high speed and hit that tree!* How true the Word of God is! *"The rod and reproof give wisdom: but a child left to* *himself bringeth his mother to shame,"* **Proverbs 29:15**. Nobody is smarter than God. Discipline is a vital part of growing up. Failure has devastating long-term consequences. Not only does the person void of self-control ultimately feel the bitter lash, but the parents feel it, the family feels it, the community feels the violence and lawlessness that accompanies it and the entire society pays: increased police and prisons, more health care for those who didn't say *"no"* to promiscuous sex or drugs, more taxes and the list seems endless.

PERSONAL DISCIPLINE IS VITAL TO CHRISTIAN MATURITY

The parallel between social maturity and Christian maturity is undeniable. God expects His people to grow increasingly mature. **2 Peter 3:18** is a command: *"But grow in grace, and in the knowledge of our Lord and Saviour Jesus Christ."* Growth stagnation is offensive to God. Listen to God's blanket rebuke of those who fail to grow up. *"For when for the time ye ought to be teachers, ye have need that one teach you again which be the first principles of the oracles of God; and are become such as have need of milk, and not of strong meat. For every one that useth milk is unskilful in the word of righteousness: for he is a babe. But strong meat belongeth to them that are of full age, even those who by reason of use have their senses exercised to discern both good and evil,"* **Hebrews 5:12-14**. Personal discipline is one of the ways in which Christian maturity manifests itself. Its absence is a glaring evidence of immaturity.

A LOOK AT WHAT PERSONAL DISCIPLINE IS

Webster's dictionary offers a quite concise definition of self-control: "Control of one's self or of one's feelings and actions." [1] A self-controlled person brings to mind thoughts of will-power, stedfastness, backbone, responsibility, dependability and the ability to resist temptation. He is a person who is disciplined, who has learned to resist evil and choose good, who recognizes danger as well as opportunity and who knows how to say *"no"* and *"yes"* at the right times. That involves wisdom, discernment and good judgment.

THE BIBLE WORD IS *"TEMPERANCE"*

Under divine inspiration the Apostle Peter said, *"Whereby are given unto us exceeding great and precious promises: that by these ye might be partakers of the divine nature, having escaped the corruption that is in the world through lust. And beside this, giving all diligence, add to your faith virtue; and to virtue knowledge; And to knowledge temperance; and to temperance patience; and to patience godliness; And to godliness brotherly kindness; and to brotherly kindness charity. For if these things be in you, and abound, they make you that ye shall neither be barren nor unfruitful in the knowledge of our Lord Jesus Christ. But he that lacketh these things is blind, and cannot see afar off, and hath forgotten that he was purged from his old sins,"* **2 Peter 1:4-9**. Notice well; get *"knowledge,"* but not for knowledge's sake. Get *"knowledge,"* but use it. It is truth applied that enables a Christian to resist what he ought to resist and embrace what he ought to embrace. Thus Peter said add *"temperance"* to *"knowledge."*

Temperance is from the Greek word egkrateia. This Greek word is a derivative of egkrates which means to be strong in anything; masterful. It is used especially when speaking of the control of fleshly appetites such as sex, food and pleasure.[2] Egkrates is a compound word. It comes from a combination of en, a primary preposition denoting a fixed position [3] and kratos which speaks of vigor (dominion and might), power and strength.[4] Note well that en is rarely used with verbs of motion. It is not a directional preposition; it connotes being at rest or stabilized. The idea of *temperance* is that of being in control, not being controlled by our own will and passions or by the environment around us including its people. Having temperance means you are settled on many important issues. You have fixed positions on the key issues of life. The Bible identifies the *key issues* of life and states the correct positions where Christians should be *fixed.*

While Paul was incarcerated at Caesarea awaiting transfer to Rome, he met with several magistrates including the local governor, Felix. His extremely godless wife Drusilla was also present. The historian Josephus [5] represents Felix as greedy for money. Earlier Felix had induced his wife Drusilla to leave her former husband Aziz, King of Emesa. It is not surprising that as Paul reasoned with him *"of righteousness, temperance, and judgment to come, Felix trembled,"* **Acts 24:25**. Greek scholar A.T. Robertson said *"was terrified"* is the literal rending of the Greek words for *trembled.* [6] Felix had no personal discipline, no self-control, no restraint of his fleshly appetites and lusts. *Temperance* hit him hard as it does large numbers of physically mature adults including professing Christians. Many of these hold high positions in churches and are held in high esteem. They are thought to be mature by others.

HOW CAN A CHRISTIAN POSSIBLY CONTROL SELF?

Since self (*"the flesh"*) is one of the greatest enemies of every child of God, **Romans 8:8**, how can self-control possibly be an earmark of Christian maturity? Not one Christian is a match for Satan who works against us through our flesh; however, Satan is no match for the Holy Spirit who lives in every believer. *"Ye are of God, little children, and have overcome them: because greater is he that is in you, than he that is in the world,"* **1 John 4:4**. When a child of God yields his spirit in submission to the indwelling Holy Spirit of God, he is under the control of the Holy Spirit. The believer is making the choices and exercising the strength and discipline to resist what he should and act in a godly manner, but not in his own wisdom and strength. He is doing so in the wisdom and strength of God. Here is how the Apostle Paul explained it. *"Not that we are sufficient of ourselves to think any thing as of ourselves; but our sufficiency is of God,"* **2 Corinthians 3:5**. He also said of Spirit-led believers, *"it is God which worketh in you both to will and to do of his good pleasure,"* **Philippians 2:13**.

Temperance in the Bible sense of the word is widely misunderstood. In no sense does the word imply that Christians in their own strength and will-power are to stand against evils (even the evil lusts of their own flesh) and walk in righteousness. No! They can't do it on their own; they don't have the power; but they can do it in the power of the Holy Spirit. In fact, when a true Christian yields to the Holy Spirit, *temperance* will be natural and automatic. The Spirit will take charge and give all the strength that is needed for the believer to obey the Word of God in any situation. Just as hair naturally grows on horses and leaves grow on trees, self-control (control by the Holy Spirit) naturally flows through the Christian yielded to the Holy Spirit. The Apostle Paul explained it this way, *"But the fruit of the Spirit is love, joy, peace, longsuffering, gentleness, goodness, faith, Meekness, temperance: against such there is no law,"* **Galatians 5:22-23**. Note it well. Like all of the other named virtues, *temperance* is automatic. Believers do not have to make it happen; *temperance* comes naturally to those who yield to the control of the Holy Spirit who lives within them. As they gain knowledge of His Word and yield to Him, He provides all the power they need for implementation. Victory and discipline come not through will-power; they come through the power of the Holy Spirit of God. Temperance is "the normal out-cropping of the Holy Spirit in us." He is the "one holding control." [7]

A MARK OF MATURITY

On this issue of growing up to maturity the Apostle Paul said, *"When I was a child, I spake as a child, I understood as a child, I thought as a child: but when I became a man, I put away childish things,"* **1 Corinthians 13:11**. There can be little doubt that one of the things he put away was his undisciplined ways. He learned to restrain and control his life, to recognize boundaries, to say *yes* to some things and *no* to others. He learned life was not all about him and his agenda. We're talking about personal discipline.

That's the way it is as people mature. We learn to recognize who is mature and who is not by how they control themselves. Regardless of one's age in years, it's pretty easy to tell the difference between a spoiled baby and a mature adult. Personal discipline or the lack thereof is a dead give-away. No Christian without *temperance* is mature, and there can be no truly successful spiritual life without it.

---

[1] *Webster's New World Dictionary with Student Handbook: Young People's Edition,* s.v. "self-control," (Nashville, Tennessee: The World Publishing Company, 1973), 628.

[2] James Strong, *Greek Dictionary of the New Testament,* (Nashville, Tennessee: Abingdon Press, 1958), reference 1468.

[3] Ibid., reference 1722.

[4] Ibid., reference 2904.

[5] Josephus was a non-Christian Jewish historian at the time of the New Testament. He has the favor of the Romans and wrote extensively on events and people of that era.

[6] A.T. Robertson, *Word Pictures in the New Testament,* vol. 3, (Nashville, Tennessee: Broadman Press, 1930), 422-423.

[7] Robertson, vol. 4, 313.

Chapter 7

Wisdom

If you'd like to hear the average person flounder all around with that *deer in the headlights* look, ask him to explain the difference between knowledge and wisdom. Most of us know at least a few people who are really smart, who have a wealth of knowledge, but who have no common sense. The dictionary says *knowledge* is the fact or condition of knowing. It is that which is known or learned through study or experience. [1] The same dictionary says *wisdom* is "the quality of being wise; good judgment that comes from knowledge and experience in life." [2] And, what is *"wise?"* It is "having or showing good judgment." [3] Oh yes, there is a vast difference between having knowledge and knowing how to harness and handle it. Solomon observed, *"As a jewel of gold in a swine's snout, so is a fair woman which is without discretion,"* **Proverbs 11:22**. There's a strong connection between wisdom and discretion, discernment, prudence, good judgment and plain ole common sense.

KNOWLEDGE WITHOUT WISDOM

To have wisdom is to know how to properly use and apply knowledge. Wisdom is not merely gaining more knowledge. The Bible speaks of those who are *"Ever learning, and never able to come to the knowledge of the truth,"* **2 Timothy 3:7**. Wisdom, which is understanding and a sense of reason, does not automatically equate with intelligentsia and academia. As godly and strong as Job was, he admitted that before his enormous trials, his great knowledge and expressions thereof were far out in front of his wisdom. *"I uttered that I understood not,"* **Job 42:3**.

Is there one among us who has not *spoken too soon*? We weighed in on a matter before we got things straight and made a fool of our self in the process. We expect that of children, especially in those adolescent years; but we expect better of adults. Sadly some people never seem to grow up. They get so caught up in their great learning that they lose sight of reality. When the Apostle Paul was incarcerated at Caesarea, Festus was the Roman governor. At one point Festus and other Roman officials asked Paul to defend himself against the charges he faced due to his Christian faith. As he did so, Festus was so smitten with what he heard that he thought Paul was a madman. **Acts 26:24** records the event. *"And as he thus spake for himself, Festus said with a loud voice, Paul, thou art beside thyself; much learning doth make thee mad."* In Paul's case the accusation was untrue, but the point is clear: great learning and knowledge do not guarantee the proper use and application thereof. Sometimes academic learning and acumen not only generate blindness, they also generate pride.

Nicodemus is another case in point. The man was a *"ruler of the Jews,"* **John 3:1**. He knew the Law and could quote great sections of the Old Testament, yet he was blind to the point of most of what he knew. The Old Testament with its Levitical Law pointed forward to the Messiah. Here was the Messiah in person standing face to face with Nicodemus, but Nicodemus didn't recognize him or have a clue about the New Birth. All of that education and scholarship did not help Nicodemus who, like most of the scholars of his day and ours, did not know what true life is or how to get it. He had knowledge, but didn't know how to use it; he didn't know how to apply what he knew.

What a sad, but common picture! Historians call this age *the enlightenment*. Greater and greater numbers of people are educated.

To compete in modern society, people need college degrees. Yet, increasingly bizarre and irrational ideas appear in the marketplace of ideas. Regardless of how foolish and out of step with truth and reality a concept may be, if it comes from a *scholar* with lots of letters at the end of his name, it is usually embraced by society as a whole, particularly by liberals.

Yes. It is possible to be very knowledgeable and scholarly and still be a fool (a person void of wisdom). Sometimes people with great educations and much knowledge are proud of it, ever ready to let you know how smart and superior they are. They are not nearly as interested in understanding and truth as they are in winning arguments and flaunting their great intellect. Solomon said, *"A fool hath no delight in understanding, but that his heart may discover itself,"* **Proverbs 18:2**.

THE PROPER APPLICATION OF KNOWLEDGE

As I progressed through the educational world, I woke up to the fact that knowledge was not an end within itself; it's a means to a higher end. The objective is not to learn numbers and how to count; we learn the basic facts in order to solve problems. Learning to count, add, subtract, multiply and divide enable us to reconcile a checkbook, determine distances, calculate prices and solve untold problems. Without the basics of math there could be no engineers, accountants and other scientists. But keep in mind that it is not the math whizzes who excel; it is those who are wise enough to harness and put to work all that knowledge. Using the facts, figures, formulas and other basic math to build bridges and buildings, to calculate all that will be needed to send a man to outer space and bring him home safely and to build a great company is the purpose of all that knowledge. The end is not in learning a language, the ABC's, grammar and reading. The objective is effective communications: using those basics to study, speak and write effectively.

Why learn the Bible? So you can be a *great scholar,* so you can *win religious arguments,* so you can *impress people with how much you know* and *how holy you are?* God forbid! You learn God's Word so that you may know Him, so you can represent Him well in this world and so that you might bring others to Him.

It's not just truth; it is truth applied that honors God. It is hard to imagine any truth being stated more clearly than this one is stated in **James 1:22-25**. *"But be ye doers of the word, and not hearers only, deceiving your own selves. For if any be a hearer of the word, and not a doer, he is like unto a man beholding his natural face in a glass: For he beholdeth himself, and goeth his way, and straightway forgetteth what manner of man he was. But whoso looketh into the perfect law of liberty, and continueth therein, he being not a forgetful hearer, but a doer of the work, this man shall be blessed in his deed."* Note well where the blessing is! The blessing goes to the *"doer of the work."* That's application. It is knowledge properly applied, not knowledge alone. That's wisdom!

Jesus spoke of this reality. He said there are those who just don't get it. They have plenty of knowledge, but they still miss the point. They think they have the answers, but they don't. *"Therefore speak I to them in parables: because they seeing see not; and hearing they hear not, neither do they understand. And in them is fulfilled the prophecy of Esaias, which saith, By hearing ye shall hear, and shall not understand; and seeing ye shall see, and shall not perceive: For this people's heart is waxed gross, and their ears are dull of hearing, and their eyes they have closed; lest at any time they should see with their eyes, and hear with their ears, and should understand with their heart, and should be converted, and I should heal them. But blessed are your eyes, for they see: and your ears, for they hear,"* **Matthew 13:13-16**.

Wisdom is getting it, understanding it, and knowing what to do with it. That involves listening. Solomon said, *"The way of a fool is right in his own eyes: but he that hearkeneth unto counsel is wise,"* **Proverbs 12:15**. He continued, *"A fool despiseth his father's instruction: but he that regardeth reproof is prudent,"* **Proverbs 15:5**.

WISDOM AND MATURITY GO TOGETHER

Regardless of how much knowledge one has, without wisdom he cannot be considered mature. In fact, his level of wisdom will generally reveal his degree of maturity. In Paul's famous rebuke of the Hebrew believers, he spoke of discernment. One of the main reasons he considered them to be *"babes"* and immature was their lack of discernment. They had little application of truth. When they should have progressed and grown to maturity, they still had to be spoon fed with a baby's diet. *"Of whom we have many things to say, and hard to be uttered, seeing ye are dull of hearing. For when for the time ye ought to be teachers, ye have need that one teach you again which be the first principles of the oracles of God; and are become such as have need of milk, and not of strong meat. For every one that useth milk is unskilful in the word of righteousness: for he is a babe. But strong meat belongeth to them that are of full age, even those who by reason of use have their senses exercised to discern both good and evil,"* **Hebrews 5:11-14**.

Does that remind you of anyone you know, maybe even you? I know people who have never learned to control their appetites or their tongues. They are not little children anymore; they're in their teens or twenties or older, but they have little discretion. They're bright and have lots of knowledge, but they don't use it very well. Grown? No! Physically mature, but mental babes! Very immature! I also know a great many Christians who have been saved for a long time. They have a head full of Bible knowledge. They know how to dot the "I" and the "T." By now you'd think they would be bastions of godly wisdom, but that is not the case. Some of them can't even give a good testimony of their own salvation, let alone lead someone to Christ. (Some of them have to run to the preacher to lead their own children to Christ.) After years very few of them have led anyone to Christ, not one soul! Apologetics or defending their faith! Forget it. The prospect of a confrontation makes their palms sweat. They can't enunciate why they believe the Bible is the divinely inspired, inerrant Word of God. They can't give solid reasons why God created the heavens and earth, and the prospect of a showdown with a Darwinian Evolutionist strikes fear in their hearts. What about the deity of

Christ, salvation by grace through faith apart from human works and the eternal security of the believer? Baptism by immersion only after salvation and by the authority of a sound church is one of the cutting-edge issues of the last two centuries. Ask most believers to explain why and they'll back up like a crayfish.

The church is a local body of baptized believers covenanted together to keep the ordinances and carry out the Great Commission; it is not a universal body. How many Christians do you know who can defend that turf? We are speaking about the most rudimentary and fundamental Christian doctrines, yet multitudes of Christians who have been saved for years have almost no knowledge of how to use these truths. And, when it comes to the practice of holiness, it's downright embarrassing. The sad fact is that based on observance, it's hard to tell the difference between a lost person and a saved person, between a week-old Christian and a forty year old Christian. What about the exercise of Christian virtues such as forgiveness, a spirit of giving, kindness, morality, treatment of others, the handling of money, conflict resolution, attitudes and values in life? Somehow too many Christians have never moved to the application of truth to daily living. Wisdom is application, not mere knowledge. It is getting the knowledge of God into your system and properly using and applying it on a routine basis.

Wisdom or the lack thereof marks one's maturity level. If your decision making ability and your application of biblical truth has not graduate past puberty, it is presumption and arrogant to think of yourself as being mature. Growing up is getting past childish reactions and poor judgments. As children grow and become more mature, they make increasingly competent decisions and judgments. They increasingly learn to effectively use the information they have learned. They become able to recognize dangers, choose that which is good and interface with other people.

Seeing these developments in our children tell us where they are in terms of growth and maturity. Likewise in Christian growth and maturity! Increasingly effective application of biblical principles in the everyday life of a believer speaks of growth and maturity. Lack of increasingly effective application of biblical principles in the everyday life of a believer speaks of immaturity. Every believer should apply what the Bible says to his attitude, his moral life, his thought life, his work ethic, his marriage, his interpersonal relationships and his worship. He should apply what the Bible says to bring people to Christ, to the use of money, to prayer and to participation in church. This kind of application testifies of maturity, but those who fail to apply the truths they know are immature. That is true regardless of how much they may know, how charismatic and mouthy they are, how much money they give, how pious they seem and how animated they may become in a church worship service. It is living testimonies that tell the tale, not posturing or pretences. Until death every Christian should be learning and applying truth. Every one of us should be continuously growing and becoming ever more mature in the Lord.

ASK

Later in this book there will be more information on how to activate and accelerate the spiritual growth process; however, at this point we must visit **James 1:5**. *"If any of you lack wisdom, let him ask of God, that giveth to all men liberally, and upbraideth not; and it shall be given him."* Ask! Yes, ask God for wisdom. God can give you wisdom. When your heart is tender, surrendered and predisposed to use and apply the truth to your life, God can give you greater and greater understanding.

Do not be deluded into thinking God is simply going to pour wisdom into your head apart from anything on your part. Our emphasis in this chapter has been on wisdom and not knowledge; however, that is not to say that knowledge is not important. It is important. Wisdom grows out of knowledge. Thus, Solomon spoke of getting both. *"Get wisdom, get understanding: forget it not;*

neither decline from the words of my mouth. Forsake her not, and she shall preserve thee: love her, and she shall keep thee. Wisdom is the principal thing; therefore get wisdom: and with all thy getting get understanding. Exalt her, and she shall promote thee: she shall bring thee to honour, when thou dost embrace her. She shall give to thine head an ornament of grace: a crown of glory shall she deliver to thee," **Proverbs 4:5-9**. Once the knowledge is there, God can help you harness it. In fact, you will gain wisdom as you study the Bible and while observing the lives of elder Christian brothers and sisters. We learn and gain wisdom from observing examples of knowledge properly applied. You see this truth in Paul's exhortation to young Timothy. *"Consider what I say; and the Lord give thee understanding in all things,"* **2 Timothy 2:7**. Paul didn't instruct Timothy to ask for wisdom from God and then do nothing. Wisdom would come from *"the Lord,"* but Timothy (and you) would have to stay in the Word of God to get it. God will only help with the raw materials you place in His hands. If you sit around waiting for him to simply pour wisdom into your head with no learning on your part, you will not get wisdom regardless of how much you ask.

King Solomon who is the wisest man to ever live is a splendid example of the link between asking for wisdom from God and getting it. Listen to his request to God for wisdom. While you are reading his prayer, also consider the heart that he had in asking. Notice also the impact that his true heart had on God. *"And now, O LORD my God, thou hast made thy servant king instead of David my father: and I am but a little child: I know not how to go out or come in. And thy servant is in the midst of thy people which thou hast chosen, a great people, that cannot be numbered nor counted for multitude. Give therefore thy servant an understanding heart to judge thy people, that I may discern between good and bad: for who is able to judge this thy so great a people? And the speech pleased the Lord, that Solomon had asked this thing. And God said unto him, Because thou hast asked this thing, and hast not asked for thyself long life; neither hast asked riches for thyself, nor hast asked the life of thine enemies; but hast asked for thyself understanding to discern judgment; Behold, I have done according to thy words: lo, I have given thee a wise and an understanding heart; so that there was none like thee before thee, neither after thee shall any arise like unto thee,"* **1 Kings 3:7-12**. That's how it's done. Out of a pure heart, you ask. And, while you wait, you study God's Word and learn from those older Christian whom God has put into your life. The wisdom will come and as it does, those around you will recognize that a wonderful transformation is occurring in your life. You're growing up, moving from a spiritual child to an adult. You are maturing!

A MORE TELLING EARMARK IS ON THE WAY

Several human characteristics speak to the issue of maturity. Some are more obvious than others. The next chapter in this book will address the rather painful issue of criticism. Talk about testing one's maturity metal, criticism will do it especially when the criticism is destructive. We will therefore examine Christian maturity from the standpoint of criticism.

---

1 *Webster's New World Dictionary with Student Handbook: Young People's Edition,* s.v. "knowledge," (Nashville, Tennessee: The World Publishing Company, 1973), 391.

2 Ibid., s.v. "wisdom," 796.

3 Ibid., s.v. "wise."

Chapter 8

Understanding Criticism

At this junction we're stepping into that proverbial no-man's-land. This place involves true friendship and it *tests the mettle* of even the strongest of God's veterans. The characteristic we're about to consider is truly one that separates the boys from the men. Criticism is a measuring device, in both its receiving and giving. As you are about to see, your handling of criticism will flush you out, tell you just how grown up you really are (or are not). In this chapter and the next, we will consider the receiving of criticism. A little later we will consider giving it. The proper handling of both aspects of criticism is an irrefutable earmark of great maturity. Failure on either end says you have a long way to go.

CRITICISM IS A REALITY OF LIFE

You will not live long apart from criticism. In fact, the older you get the more you will be criticized. That's particularly true as you increasingly make a difference in the world around you. The higher you rise in leadership and influence, the more you will face criticism and the more intense it will become. Visit a presidential library. There will be a section given to the president's critics and the criticism he received. What you read may shock you: vile stuff, oozing hatred, death threats. When it comes to critics, nothing is sacred and there are no restraints. Presidents, preachers, parents and patriots all get it; and you will too. In fact, the more you give yourself to God and serving Him, the more you will be questioned, castigated and condemned. Critics eventually murdered Jesus Christ.

The dictionary says a critic is "a person who is quick to find fault." [1] The world is full of *arm-chair generals* who will jump at the chance to pass judgment on you. Most of them have no decent résumé of their own, but they can tell you what you should do and how you should do it. They usually have no proven plan, but they will pick your plan to pieces. In spite of God's prohibition against it, many of them will judge your heart and your motives.

Usually criticism is harsh, rude and destructive. It can be constructive; but the majority of people take a strange and rather sadistic pleasure in being cruel and hurting other people. There's something about putting people down and conquering others that seems to give a sense of importance, power and mastery to many. Masses of people feed on being negative, critical and against almost everything. They mean their criticism for bad; however, God can turn it to your good. Old Testament Joseph expressed this reality when he said to his critical brothers, *"ye thought evil against me; but God meant it unto good,"* **Genesis 50:20**.

CRITICISM CAN HELP YOU

It is very rare for anyone to respond positively to criticism. The common response is negative. We get mad and strike back. *How dare him; he needs to clean up his own back yard. He's a hypocrite; let me tell you what's wrong with him.* Generally when people feel under attack, they lash back. They also feel hurt. Discouragement is common. It is not uncommon for people to abandon their dreams and plans and give up. Criticism has ended many friendships and made countless enemies. The usual response to criticism is to ignore the criticism and silence the critic; however, it is wise to evaluate the big picture. God may have sent a critic to help you.

A Weakness

Your critic may be God's means of identifying a weakness in you. We all have flaws and weaknesses; lots of them; and they hurt us. They hold us back and rob us of our potential and usefulness to God. A person who is habitually late earns scorn and sometimes loses his job. In the marketplace, sloppy work and a lack of dependability keep people from advancing. People quit trusting a gossip. A preacher with poor sermons and delivery hurts himself and his church. Few people want to be around a person with a pessimistic, gloomy, critical attitude and spirit. Laziness, sarcasm, selfishness, holding grudges, hot tempers, wandering eyes and a failure to take care of responsibilities often produce divorces.

We are usually blind to our weaknesses, but a critic isn't. They see and point them out. Sometimes they point them out directly to our face; more often they point them out to someone behind our back. (We get the word second-hand, and that makes the pain and resentment worse.) Occasionally the criticism is constructive; many times it is destructive. The delivery may be unorthodox and the message may be harsh and cruel, but the critic has identified our problem, flaw or weakness.

Strangely, we pay doctors lots of money to find out what's wrong with us, but we damn and curse the critic who does it for free.

Strengthening You

God not only uses critics to help us identify our weaknesses, He also uses them to strengthen us. For those willing to face the truth about their weaknesses and humble themselves before God, criticism can be a turning point. It puts them on the road to recovery. Even when the criticism is not true, we can grow stronger as a result of the experience. Job who went through intense criticism from his *friends* said, *"When he hath tried me, I shall come forth as gold,"* **Job 23:10**. Trials have a way of strengthening people. *"Blessed is the man that endureth temptation: for when he is tried,* *he shall receive the crown of life, which the Lord hath promised to them that love him,"* **James 1:12**.

DON'T SILENCE YOUR CRITICS

Each incident of criticism is a test. It can defeat you or it can strengthen you. The potential for both is there. Response determines which way it will be. Your response to criticism should never be governed by whether or not the criticism is constructive or destructive. Most of us have the notion that if the criticism is constructive and given in love, we'll possibly listen. The truth is that some of the best, clearest, most needed criticism may come very cruelly and hatefully. Determining how much is true and working through it to victory is one of life's toughest tests especially when the criticism is cruel and hateful; but the benefits far offset the anguish. It really doesn't matter how criticism comes or from whom. Your response should always be the same. Take and use the part that is valid to grow and improve. Disregard the rest.

Those whose immediate response to criticism is negative do themselves a disservice. In the vast majority of cases criticism can help you. It has the power to identify a flaw that is hurting you and holding you back, to turn you from a bad direction that can result in a major train-wreck in your life and put you on the road to a much better life.

THE CRITIC IN YOUR LIFE MAY BE A MESSENGER FROM GOD

It never seems to occur to some of us that God has a great variety of ways by which he can communicate His Word to us. Our narrow concept thinks only in terms of reading it right out of the Bible, having it directly quoted or hearing it in a sermon or Sunday school lesson. Getting it straight from the Bible is great, but do not think God has no other ways to deliver His message to you. He may deliver it to you through a tract, a radio broadcast or through the mouth of your wife or son. You may overhear a co-worker who is not even talking to you, be quietly watching television or be reading a book. Suddenly a truth slips into your heart! You know it is right. It reminds you of what your dear mother said many years ago or of a message that convicted you to the core. Do not forget that God used a jackass to deliver a message to Balaam, **Numbers 22**, fingers writing on a wall with no voice to get his word to a Babylonian king, **Daniel 5**, the Witch of Endor to get His message to hard-hearted King Saul, **1 Samuel 28**, and a rooster to get His message to Simon Peter, **Matthew 26:74-75**.

The critic whom God uses to deliver the message will probably not realize that he is being used of God. He simply had something on his mind and said it. That's all, just made a comment or crack; got it off his chest and went on about his business; but the message reaches us. It was exactly what God wanted us to know at the time. Two unconverted Midianites shared their dream. They were oblivious to the nearby presence of Gideon; however, what they shared was exactly what God wanted Gideon to hear, **Judges 7:13-15**. After the Exodus, Moses' father-in-law Jethro visited Moses in the wilderness camp. Jethro talked about Moses' workload and lack of organization. It was a message from God, **Exodus 18**. Rebellious King Saul took hold of Samuel's garment which rent. It was a message that God was rending the kingdom of Israel from Saul and his family, **1 Samuel 15:24-29**.

Do not misunderstand what is being said here. In no sense am I saying that God is going to give you some new revelation apart from the Bible, the written Word of God. No! Never! There is no other written message from God outside the Bible. It alone is the divinely inspired, inerrant Word of God. It is finished and God has cursed all who would add to or subtract from it, **Revelation 22:18-19**. This is not a look at what truth is; it is a look at how God can get His truth to you. We're considering His delivery system. To address an issue that is hurting us, He can use even an enemy to call it to our attention. He has limitless ways to deliver to us the great truths which are written in His book. At the exact moment when we need to be reminded of a specific truth, He can use someone standing close by (or a thousand other ways) to bring it to our attention.

Every one of these is a messenger from God to deliver to you some aspect of truth that He has already revealed in His written Word, the Bible. He's not trying to tell you something new; He's reminding you of His truth through a critic. He's using a human instrument to pierce your spiritual ear with His message.

WE ARE NOT PEOPLE OF CHANCE OR ACCIDENT

Our God is a God of design and order. Every law of physics stands in mute testimony to this truth. The Apostle Paul said, *"And we know that all things work together for good to them that love God, to them who are the called according to his purpose,"* **Romans 8:28**. Every person who enters your life is there by design, not by accident. God either sent or allowed that person to cross your path, and that person may be God's special instrument or messenger to deliver His specific message of truth to you. That person will probably never realize God used him. He may not believe there is a God much less want to be used by Him. He may not carry out his messenger job very well; and he may deliver it in a harsh, cruel and cold way. None of that really matters. If God has a message for you, regardless of how He delivers it to you and in spite of the messenger, you'd better be listening.

It is the intent of God to penetrate our attention with His message of truth which we so badly need. The point is the message, not the delivery system. It matters not whether it comes through a friend, husband, wife, son or daughter or through a lost person. I suspect that every day God has a parade of important messengers passing through our lives with messages we desperately need to correct and turn us from trouble and destruction. Sadly we're blind to the messengers and ignore most of them. We have no idea God is remotely involved with them. It seems like *random chance*, a coincidence or the natural flow of life. We see no message from God and do not realize God has sent a messenger. A mature Christian does not believe in *random chance* or coincidence for God to get His message to us.

There are harsh consequences for those who turn a deaf ear to God. *"And ye have forgotten the exhortation which speaketh unto you as unto children, My son, despise not thou the chastening of the Lord, nor faint when thou art rebuked of him: For whom the Lord loveth he chasteneth, and scourgeth every son whom he receiveth. If ye endure chastening, God dealeth with you as with sons; for what son is he whom the father chasteneth not?"* **Hebrews 12:5-7**. Those who turn a deaf ear to God's efforts to correct their flaws and weaknesses open themselves to severe discipline: broken relationships such as marriages and friendships, disappointments, bitterness, economic bondage, business failures, broken health and even premature death.

Pay attention. Don't write off anybody, even your enemies, before you hear what they have to say. *"He that answereth a matter before he heareth it, it is folly and shame unto him,"* **Proverbs 18:13**. Always keep your head in the game. God wants growth and spiritual prosperity for you. He will not stand idly by while you have a debilitating, crippling flaw to which you are blind. Often He will send a critic into your life. He will give you a wake-up call; help you see what you didn't voluntarily see. It's easy to get mad about it and refuse to get the message. If you ignore the truth about yourself and continue in the same old way, you can expect lots of escalating trouble: heartache, defeat, barrenness.

2 Samuel 16 records a very interesting story. King David had committed a very heinous sin. The Lord was taking him off his throne. His own son was leading a rebellion and David was fleeing for his life. As he came down the rocky steeps out of Jerusalem an old enemy named *"Shimei, the son of Gera"* came forth and cursed David. Talk about criticize and condemn, Shimei took it to a new level. One of David's mightiest soldiers was enraged and pleaded with David for vengeance. *"Why should this dead dog* *curse my lord the king? let me go over, I pray thee, and take off his head,"* **2 Samuel 16:9**. In the next two verses David reached one of the highest pinnacles in his life. *"And the king said, What have I to do with you, ye sons of Zeruiah? so let him curse, because the LORD hath said unto him, Curse David. Who shall then say, Wherefore hast thou done so? And David said to Abishai, and to all his servants, Behold, my son, which came forth of my bowels, seeketh my life: how much more now may this Benjamite do it? let him alone, and let him curse; for the LORD hath bidden him,"* **2 Samuel 16:10-11**. David got the message. It came rude, crude and cruel, but he got it. Oh, how all of us need to get hold of this lesson in criticism!

Not one of us can afford to grow hard and insensitive. Our hearts must ever remain tilled soil, always open to the message of God, regardless of how it reaches us. Wise Solomon said, *"Keep thy foot when thou goest to the house of God, and be more ready to hear, than to give the sacrifice of fools: for they consider not that they do evil,"* **Ecclesiastes 5:1**. In the New Testament the Apostle James echoed that sentiment. *"Wherefore, my beloved brethren, let every man be swift to hear, slow to speak, slow to wrath: For the wrath of man worketh not the righteousness of God,"* **James 1:19-20**. That's God's idea about it: listen and keep open your ears and heart. Don't get hard and deaf and allow yourself to ignore the messengers and messages God sends to you.

THERE IS MORE TO COME ON THIS SUBJECT

This chapter has been about critics and criticism. We are not through with that subject. In the next chapter of this book we will look at how to use criticism to your advantage. It's painful, but it works. We will see how to distinguish criticism that is valid from that which is not. We will also see how determined Satan uses criticism to your destruction. Best of all we will see how to turn valid criticism to victory.

Those who learn this lesson are the grown-ups. Yes, it takes maturity to properly deal with criticism.

---

[1] *Webster's New World Dictionary with Student Handbook: Young People's Edition, s.v. "critic,"* (Nashville, Tennessee: The World Publishing Company, 1973), 170.

Chapter 9

Turning Criticism into Victory

"The ear that heareth the reproof of life abideth among the wise. He that refuseth instruction despiseth his own soul: but he that heareth reproof getteth understanding," **Proverbs 15:31-32**.

It is one thing to know in your heart that criticism can be beneficial; it is altogether another thing to deal with it in a constructive manner. Each incident of criticism is a test with the potential to either defeat or strengthen you. Response determines which it will be. (Read that line again, and let its truth sink deep into your heart.)

Your response to criticism should never be governed by whether or not the criticism is constructive or destructive. Most of us have the notion that we'll listen if it is constructive and given in love. The truth is that some of your best, clearest and most needed criticism may come very cruelly and hatefully. It really doesn't matter from whom or how criticism arrives. Your personal response to it should always be the same: do not reject it before you consider its validity.

Facing criticism and working through it to victory is one of the toughest tests you'll ever face, especially when the criticism is cruel and hateful. It is a painful spiritual exercise. Most people are too immature to do it; but until a believer can consistently work through criticism in a positive way, he is still lacking full maturity.

Criticism often defeats people. When it comes many react in anger. They view it as a personal attack. It shakes their self-esteem and confidence. It is common for people to react with discouragement, resentment and even bitterness and revenge. Satan capitalizes on it to wreck and destroy people. He is persistent. Just because one's initial response to criticism may be good does not mean victory has been won. Victory over criticism is the result of a process rather than a single decision or event. The process is somewhat like a road with several junctions. Each junction offers two options which lead in an opposing direction. Taking the wrong option always leads to defeat and disaster. Taking the correct or right option turns your direction away from the flaw or issue that unaddressed has the potential to greatly handicap or completely ruin you.

Between the time a valid criticism enters into your life and true victory over it, there are four distinct junctions or crossroads. When the road is correctly negotiated, it becomes what I call *the victory road over criticism.*

Junction 1

COMPLETE REJECTION VERSUS CONSIDERATION OF ITS VALIDITY

Somehow a criticism reaches you. It may be direct, straight from the critic. It may arrive indirectly, second-hand via a letter, a friend or a rumor. Criticism does not often arrive directly. As we shall see in our next chapter, it is risky to offer criticism; most people are afraid to offer criticism. Furthermore, criticism may be given lovingly and constructively; however, it may be given hatefully, destructively and cruelly. How it arrives and whether or not it comes lovingly and constructively or hatefully and destructively is not what's most important. What is most important is that it reached you. When it does you are faced with two options and possible responses.

Option 1: Rejection and Refusal to Consider It

This is the defeat option and response. This is exactly what most of us instinctively do. Immediate rejection! We do not even think about whether or not it is valid especially if it comes from an enemy or in a harsh way. The criticism rolls off us like water off a duck's back. It may in fact be absolutely valid and just exactly what we need to correct our lives, but that possibility never occurs to us. The criticism never gets a chance to be heard: to rise or fall on its merits.

Like most people it is most likely that you receive lots of mail. There is probably a category you don't even open: the kind that says *"Resident,"* the form letters; what we call *junk mail.* I must admit there have been times when mail I received went straight to the garbage. I didn't even open the envelope. It could have had hundreds of dollars inside, but I'll never know. I never opened the mail.

That's exactly how it is with most criticism. We just throw it away; never consider that it might have merit or validity. Usually criticism makes us mad, and the first thing we do is find something wrong in our critic and start criticizing him. *"You tell me that I am cold, indifferent and rude. Well, you fatso, you've got the gall. Your breath stinks and you hog conversations." "My wife tells me that I'm not a spiritual leader. Buddy, have you seen how rebellious and un-submissive she is?"* Yes, one of the most common of all responses to criticism is to immediately strike back. Like a jack-in-the box your mind begins a parade of what's wrong with your critic. We say he's judgmental, boast about how glad we are that God is our judge, and that the judgment of men really doesn't matter. (The truth is that the criticism tears us up on the inside.)

Anger blinds and ruins! No wonder Solomon wrote, *"He that is slow to anger is better than the mighty; and he that ruleth his spirit than he that taketh a city,"* **Proverbs 16:32**. More than any other factor, anger causes us to take the first wrong turn in responding to criticism.

Failure to consider the validity of the criticism slams shut the door to correction of the flaw at which the criticism was leveled. It kills our chances of correcting and overcoming the flaw and sets us up for more and harsher criticism.

Diagnosis of problems is the first step toward their correction. Often your critic has diagnosed your problem. We pay doctors to do that, yet curse our critics who do it for free. How odd! In many cases your critic has done you a great service: but if you refuse to even consider what he has said, you are going to stay right where you are, probably to your anguish, wreckage and ruin. Solomon said, *"He that refuseth instruction despiseth his own soul,"* **Proverbs 15:32**. He also said, *"He is in the way of life that keepeth instruction: but he that refuseth reproof erreth,"* **Proverbs 10:17**, and *"Whoso loveth instruction loveth knowledge: but he that hateth reproof is brutish,"* **Proverbs 12:1**. The Hebrew word is <u>ba'ar</u> meaning stupid or foolish. [1]

Rejection and refusal to consider the validity of the criticism that reaches you will leave a possible cancer in your life unaddressed. It will lock you into where you are and can lead to your ultimate defeat. Solomon warned, *"Poverty and shame shall be to him that refuseth instruction: but he that regardeth reproof shall be honoured,"* **Proverbs 13:18**. He continued, *"Correction is grievous unto him that forsaketh the way: and he that hateth reproof shall die,"* **Proverbs 15:10**. Don't take the rejection option. He is *"a fool"* who *"despiseth his father's instruction,"* **Proverbs 15:5**. Rejection of reproof or criticism is always a bad choice.

Option 2: Consider Its Validity and Merit

Whenever criticism comes your way, don't be so hasty. Don't let pride and anger blind you. Open the envelope; consider its contents. There may be a message there that can radically change your life for the better. Remember what Solomon said, *"He that refuseth reproof erreth,"* **Proverbs 10:17**.

The criticism may not be true, but you won't know that until you consider it. If you consider it and it is not true, just forget it! That's right; just forget it. Don't lose a wink of sleep over it. Don't get mad at and criticize your critic. Just forget it and go on!

It may be true. Your critic may be right, and you do yourself a favor to at least see if it is true. If it is, you now know it, and are in a position to do something about it. The Lord may have directed your critic to point out your need. As we are about to see, in the long run heeding such reproof can do you a world of good. This is the victory option.

Junction 2

DENIAL VERSUS FACING THE VALIDITY AND EXTENT OF THE IDENTIFIED PROBLEM

You are now past the first crossroads. You have at least considered what has been said, but Satan is persistent. You had to admit that there is some truth to the criticism. At this junction it is easy to be proud of yourself because you were man enough to hear your critic without anger and retaliation and honest enough to admit that he was right. What a mistake! Satan knows that now you are facing another junction with two options: a defeat option and a victory option. He will do his best to make you choose the defeat option at this second junction.

Option 1: Denial and Rejection of Its Seriousness

At this point the temptation is to minimize your mistake, flaw or offensive character. Yes, you know there is some truth to what has been said, but you reject the idea that it could be as bad as your critic said it is. He said you are a selfish wretch. You admit that a time or two your old self-will did come out pretty strong, but you refuse to see that you have to have your way in almost every area of your life. It's your money, your marriage, your church and your happiness. You are wrapped up in you and what you want, and you seldom seriously consider the needs or ideas of anyone else. You butt-in when other people are talking, never do anything where you don't stand to directly benefit; and always have to be in the limelight and the center of attention. When your critic said you were a selfish wretch, you heard him; but just barely. You got just enough to convince yourself you are really listening to criticism; but you fell far short of the weight of reality as to how you really are. The true picture your critic was communicating didn't reach you.

Don't limit yourself to a twig when someone is trying to show you a forest! If you do, you're whipped. Never minimize the extent of your flaw. Stay out of the excuse and self-justification business. It's greed; selfishness; laziness; lack of vision; pride; ego; sarcastic spirits; negative attitudes; spirits of anger; tendencies to be hasty and impatient; domineering ways; lustful; materialistic tendencies; and such like that defeat us in life. Paul said, *"For if ye live after the flesh, ye shall die: but if ye through the Spirit do mortify the deeds of the body, ye shall live,"* **Romans 8:13**. He wrote also, *"Mortify therefore your members which are upon the earth; fornication, uncleanness, inordinate affection, evil concupiscence, and covetousness, which is idolatry: For which things' sake the wrath of God cometh on the children of disobedience,"* **Colossians 3:5-6**.

On the road of criticism there are many options. If you take this option of rejecting and denying the reality of where you are and justifying yourself in the areas where you are under attack, you will never overcome the cancerous flaw that is hurting you. The long-range result will be misery, defeat and your undoing. Who is there among us that does not have a bag full of stories about good people we've personally known who have suffered and suffered and suffered because they wouldn't believe the extent of their flaws and mistakes? We could tell about a domineering wife who denies she is that bad or about an intolerant, unforgiving family which sees itself as very forgiving and understanding. Most of us know an extremely egotistical pastor who argued that he wasn't that way while he lost his church and family. We know a hot-tempered husband who gets red in the face while arguing that he doesn't have a temper problem. We're talking about people who have had enough criticism to straighten out a crooked road; and who admit there is a problem, but who basically deny and reject the extent of it. This is the defeat option or response.

Option 2: Face the Reality and Extent of Your Problem

There is another option: face the extent and true reality of your problem. Yes! Be honest about it. Don't inflate the problem beyond what it really is, but for your own sake do not deflate or minimize it. I recommend that you revisit chapter 4 in this book. The truth liberates the soul. Jesus said, *"Ye shall know the truth, and the truth shall make you free,"* **John 8:32**. Don't try to justify yourself and somehow get around the truth. Let the criticism be a springboard to you to truly probe and examine yourself in this area. *"But let a man examine himself,"* **1 Corinthians 11:28**. What wonderful, practical, heavenly advice!

King David prayed, *"Search me, O God, and know my heart: try me, and know my thoughts: And see if there be any wicked way in me, and lead me in the way everlasting,"* **Psalm 139:23-24**. It may be that God has done just that with you. He has searched you and found a major area of evil that is in the process of ruining you, and has sent a critic to you to point it out. If you'll let the reality of what he's saying soak into your soul, there's hope for you. You can win. Victory can be yours; but it won't be that way unless you are truly honest, and face the extent and reality of your problem. The writer of Psalm 119 said, *"I thought on my ways, and turned my feet unto thy testimonies,"* **Psalm 119:59**. There will be no *turning of "my feet"* until there is *"thought on my ways."* When the criticism pierces your attention, think about it. Don't be too quick to minimize the problem within you which has been exposed. Don't dismiss the matter from your mind until you have done your homework. Think it through and face what is really there. That is the way to victory.

Junction 3

SPIRITUAL SUICIDE VERSUS DETERMINATION TO CORRECT THE PROBLEM

So, now you are a big boy, a big girl. You've done what most people never do; you've both faced the criticism and found it valid and admitted that you have a serious problem. Good for you, but the victory is not yet won. The problem is still there; it remains unresolved. If you stay where you are, it will keep hurting you and it may ultimately destroy you. Satan knows that and is thus around to make sure you don't stay on the victory road over criticism. He knows that you are at another junction which presents him another opportunity to defeat you.

Option 1: Discouragement and Spiritual Suicide

Opening your eyes to the truth especially about yourself can be a rude awakening and very depressing. It's hard to face the fact that you've been an irresponsible, hardheaded failure. You've been a troublemaker and have been the source of great misery and hurt to so many. You have caused much destruction and made a heel of yourself. You look into the faces of your own mate, children and parents; and there's the hurt and bitterness; you know you put it there. Yes, a wake-up to truth and reality can be heartbreaking and depressing. The effects of pride, laziness, impatience, anger, misplaced priorities, selfishness, lust, stinginess and such are broken homes, hatred, guilt, resentments, divided churches, bitterness, defeated pastors, psychiatrists, many dollars wasted, heartache, grief, and early graves.

Every now and then (not very often) someone faces up to himself. Of these, some despair. They think there's no hope for them. They reason that they are too bad; not good for anyone or anything anymore. I've known several pastors who quit preaching; within the last few years two of them committed physical suicide. Teachers quit teaching, members drop out of church, husbands and wives give up on reconciling their marriage, people decide they cannot quit smoking, kids decide they're never going to amount to anything. They commit mental suicide; they give up, quit. Satan wins, defeat occurs. They saw the problem, realized its gravity; and rather than correct it, they gave up. Sad, really sad!

Sin and failure that is recognized but unaddressed does that to people. James said, *"But every man is tempted, when he is drawn away of his own lust, and enticed. Then when lust hath conceived, it bringeth forth sin: and sin, when it is finished, bringeth forth death,"* **James 1:14-15**. Esau is a good example. He was wrong. His values were not right. He sold his birthright for one meal, a mess of pottage. Later, he realized what he had done, yet did nothing to change his values. The result was great grief and bitterness. **Hebrews 12:16-17** relates the story. As good as truly recognizing yourself for what you are, it is not enough. Taking the turn into grief, depression and spiritual suicide is to lose in defeat at the hands of criticism.

Option 2: Determine to Correct Your Problem

At this junction the right thing to do is determine by the grace of God to correct the problem. This is the victory option. Believer, sin and its cruel effects do not have to conquer you. By correct and humble responses to God's efforts to bring your weakness to your attention, you can conquer instead of being conquered. *"Sin shall not have dominion over you,"* **Romans 6:14**. Regardless of how long your problem has been there and regardless of the stranglehold it has on you, you can correct it. Yes! You can! The Spirit of God who lives in you guarantees it. *"Ye are of God, little children, and have overcome them: because greater is he that is in you, than he that is in the world,"* **1 John 4:4**.

If you give in to pity and despair, your weakness and sin will stomp you into the ground; but if you determine by the grace of God to be a conqueror and champion over your sin and weakness, you are on the road to victory. *"We are more than conquerors through him that loved us,"* **Romans 8:37**.

Friend, I challenge you: choose victory and not defeat. Keep choosing the right options. Don't ignore criticism; consider its validity. Don't lie to yourself and minimize your problem; face the truth about its extent. Don't take the coward's way and commit spiritual suicide; in your heart determine to correct the problem. Stay on the road to victory by choosing the right options.

Junction 4

GOOD INTENTIONS VERSUS STEPS TO CORRECT THE PROBLEM

You're getting there, but you haven't arrived just yet. Now you are at another junction, one with both defeat and victory options.

Option 1: Good Intentions

It has been said that *"The road to hell is paved with good intentions."* At this point the topic is not heaven and hell, but you get the point. As good as good intentions are, they alone are not good enough. Apart from *follow-through,* good intentions are quite worthless. It is not enough to say, *"I will."* Victory comes only in doing what was willed. Paul said it takes more than a willing mind. It takes doing. A year earlier the Corinthians had promised financial help. He wrote them a letter saying it was now time for them to do what they said they would do. *"Now therefore perform the doing of it; that as there was a readiness to will, so there may be a performance also out of that which ye have. For if there be first a willing mind, it is accepted according to that a man hath, and not according to that he hath not,"* **2 Corinthians 8:11-12**.

Plans without performance are always a nasty problem. Procrastination, putting off that which should be done now! We will not be judged on the basis of what we intended to do, but rather on the basis of what we did. If you don't do it, what you intended to do won't matter. Good intentions never corrected a thing; and in spite of your good intentions, your flaw or problem will keep playing havoc with your life until you correct it. Until you actually address and correct the matter, your good intentions will not help you at all.

Option 2: Steps to Correct the Problem

This is the option that assures victory. That's right! Short of this point nothing else matters very much. Those previous steps simply put you into position to do something about your problem.

Oh, seriously addressing your flaws, weaknesses and poor character traits is so hard! The old flesh rebels. It wants to go on in its same old life-defeating way. Change is painful. And humiliating! It's not easy to say, *"I've been wrong, and I'm sorry."* Changing for the better is hard work! So often it takes a long, long time; old habits do not die easily or quickly. We seem to take two steps forward and one backward; and it's so hard to be patient and wait upon the Lord. We want to be healed of our sickness right now!

Sometimes correcting the problem means seeking counsel. That's humiliating to the ego. Staying on track requires vigilance and constant self-evaluation. It may mean getting special training. It will most likely mean the help of friends, and you may have to work on it for the rest of your life.

It will surely mean lots of prayer, leaning on the Lord and implementation of His principles. Yes! Implementation of His principles! God will not do for you what He has given you to do for yourself. Hear it for yourself. *"But whoso looketh into the perfect law of liberty, and continueth therein, he being not a forgetful hearer, but a doer of the work, this man shall be blessed in his deed,"* **James 1:25**. Don't miss it! It's the *"doer of the work"* who can expect to *"be blessed in his deed."* It is not uncommon to hear some super-pious (but highly mistaken) soul say, *"I'm going to simply trust God to take this problem from me!"* God *gives the increase*, but we have to *plant* and *water*, **1 Corinthians 3:6-7**. It is truth applied that brings about change for the better; and the initiative for applying truth is on us, not God.

Naomi ignored God and did what she and her husband wanted to do. She left Bethlehem where she should have stayed and went to Moab where she never should have gone. God exposed her stubborn, self-willed heart. Ultimately she faced the truth about herself and determined to go back to Bethlehem-Judah. **Ruth 1:19** makes a remarkable statement. It says she *"went until"* she *"came to Bethlehem."* She didn't merely decide to go and keep comforting herself that she had every intention of going. She put feet to her plans. She actually went. She stayed on the road until she got there. The prodigal son exemplified the same truth, the necessity of follow-through. *"He arose, and came to his father,"* **Luke 15:20**.

There is a road to victory over criticism, but there is no victory unless we get on the road and stay there. Satan ever seeks to turn us aside to defeat all along the way; but we choose the options, not him. Proper response to criticism is a definite characteristic of Christian maturity. Those who consistently turn criticism into growth are living examples of great maturity.

IT IS ONE THING TO PROPERLY RECEIVE CRITICISM, IT IS QUITE ANOTHER TO PROPERLY GIVE IT

A serious look at what the Bible says about giving criticism (reproof) might surprise you. It's there, in abundance. At best the giving of criticism is a tedious undertaking, but God expects us to do it. Before attempting to do so, it is a good idea to learn the right way to do it. The next chapter in this book will deal with the giving of criticism.

---

[1] James Strong, *Greek Dictionary of the New Testament,* (Nashville, Tennessee: Abingdon Press, 1958), reference 1198.

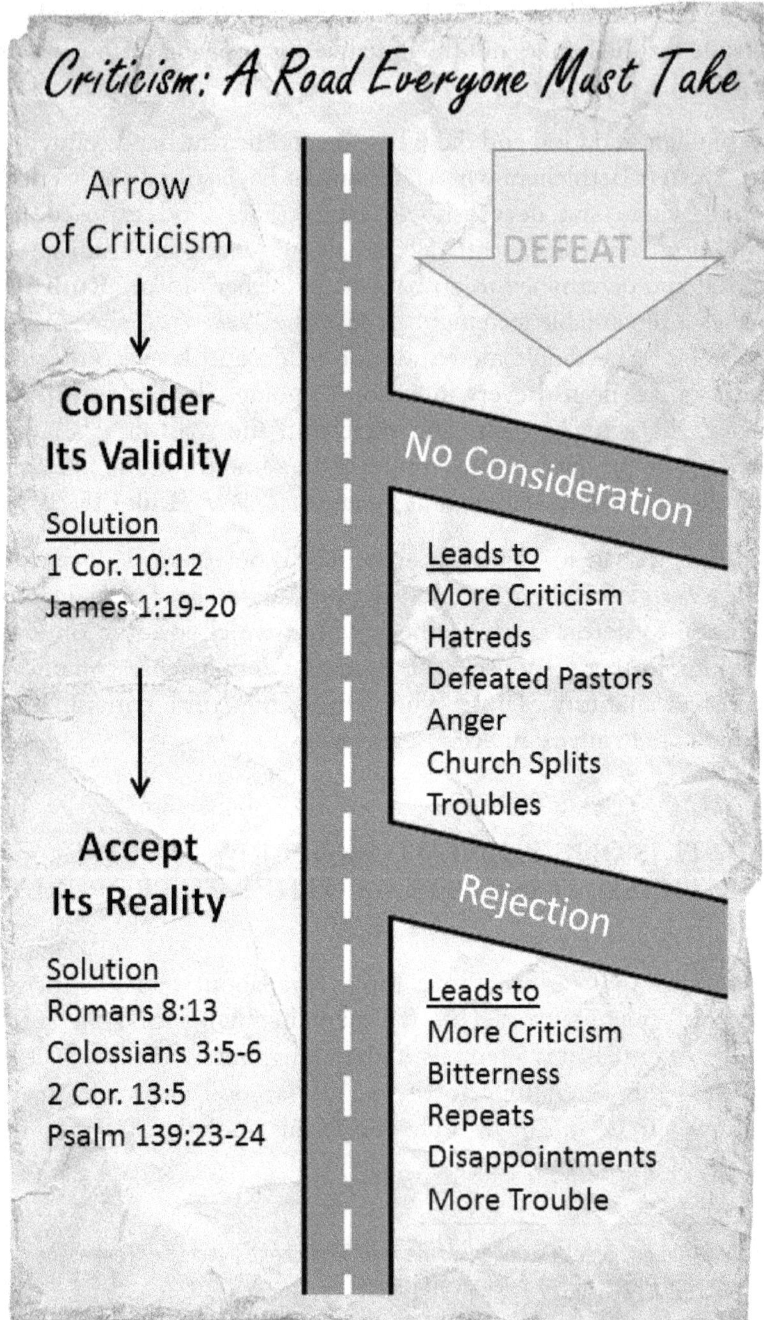
Criticism: A Road Everyone Must Take
Arrow
of Criticism
Consider
Its Validity
Solution
1 Cor. 10:12
James 1:19-20
Accept
Its Reality
Solution
Romans 8:13
Colossians 3:5-6
2 Cor. 13:5
Psalm 139:23-24
DEFEAT
No Consideration
Leads to
More Criticism
Hatreds
Defeated Pastors
Anger
Church Splits
Troubles
Rejection
Leads to
More Criticism
Bitterness
Repeats
Disappointments
More Trouble

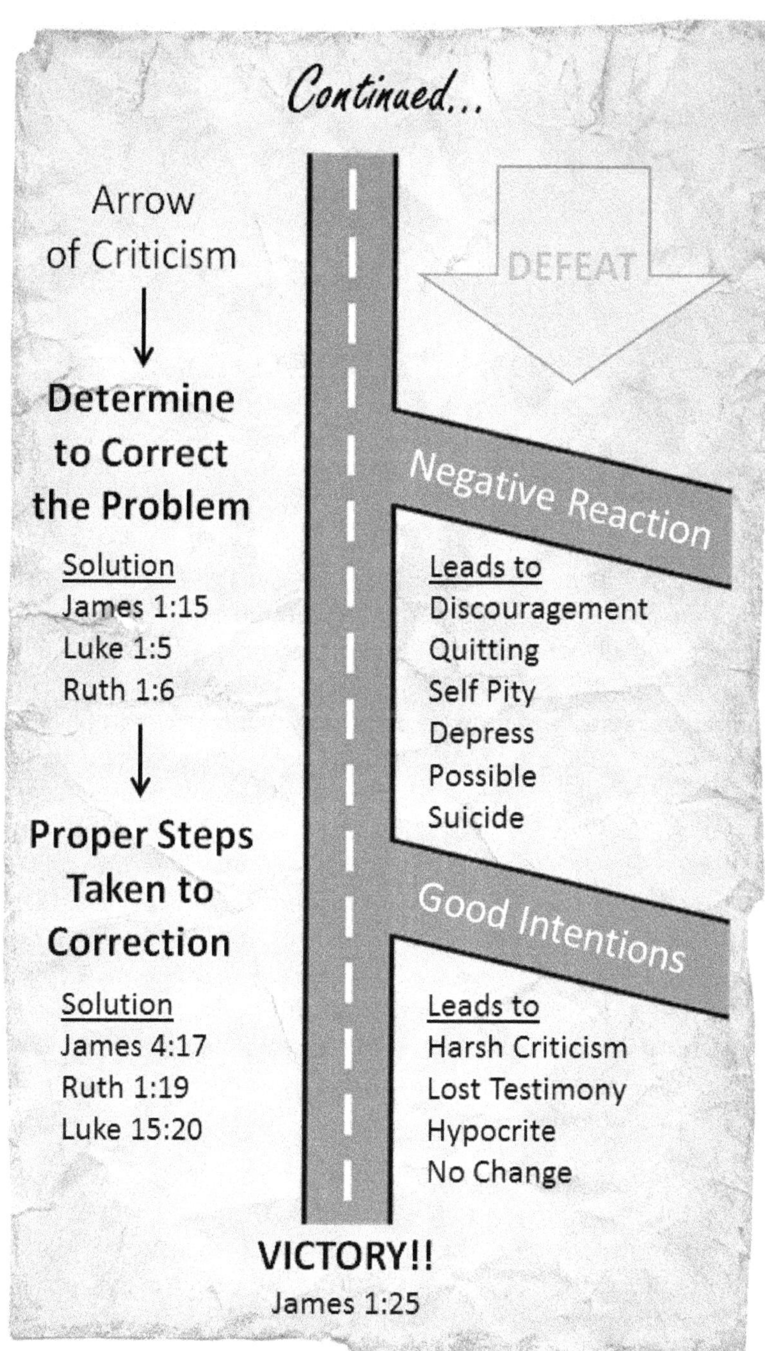
Continued...
Arrow
of Criticism
Determine
to Correct
the Problem
Solution
James 1:15
Luke 1:5
Ruth 1:6
Proper Steps
Taken to
Correction
Solution
James 4:17
Ruth 1:19
Luke 15:20
DEFEAT
Negative Reaction
Leads to
Discouragement
Quitting
Self Pity
Depress
Possible
Suicide
Good Intentions
Leads to
Harsh Criticism
Lost Testimony
Hypocrite
No Change
VICTORY!!
James 1:25

Chapter 10

Faithful Wounds of Criticism

Criticism is much, much easier to give than to take, but it is not easier to give it the right way. Most of the good critics in the world could all stand on a pinhead at one time. It bears repeating that the world is full of arm-chair generals, Monday morning quarterbacks and others who are more than ready to give their lofty and unsolicited opinions (usually without depth of consideration). There is an old piece of wisdom which says, *"It is better to be silent and be thought a fool than to open your mouth and remove all doubt."* The Bible states it this way, *"He that answereth a matter before he heareth it, it is folly and shame unto him,"* **Proverbs 18:13**. Mature people think before they criticize. *"The heart of the righteous studieth to answer: but the mouth of the wicked poureth out evil things"* **Proverbs 15:28**. Oh yes, even mature people have lapses. Unfortunately at times they speak out of character especially under stress and provocation; however, restraint and caution are among their characteristics.

Critics should keep in mind that those who live by the sword shall die by the sword. If you're going to give it, you're going to get it; and the more you give, the more you'll get. In spite of the fact that in Christ there is a higher standard, the fact is that the old Levitical standard still prevails in the general populace. *"Breach for breach, eye for eye, tooth for tooth: as he hath caused a blemish in a man, so shall it be done to him again,"* **Leviticus 24:20**.

Another piece of old wisdom says, *"Those who throw stones should not live in glass houses."* People scorn hypocrites. Before you criticize another person, look in your own mirror. Clean up your own room and get rid of your own baggage. Jesus personally addressed this issue. *"And why beholdest thou the mote that is in thy brother's eye, but perceivest not the beam that is in thine own eye? Either how canst thou say to thy brother, Brother, let me pull out the mote that is in thine eye, when thou thyself beholdest not the beam that is in thine own eye? Thou hypocrite, cast out first the beam out of thine own eye, and then shalt thou see clearly to pull out the mote that is in thy brother's eye,"* **Luke 6:41-42**.

Giving criticism properly is very difficult. If given correctly, it is much harder to give than to take. You have the power to control how you will respond to criticism; you have no power to control how the one you criticize will respond. You can rest assured that in almost 100 percent of the cases where you do not practice the ultimate care and excellence in offering criticism, it will be met with total resistance and extreme hostility and resentment. In the process, you are very likely to create an enemy for life. Twice Solomon warned, *"The words of a talebearer are as wounds, and they go down into the innermost parts of the belly,"* **Proverbs 18:8, 26:22**. Words can hurt and criticism can cut the spirit like a knife cuts the body. They wound.

Thus, we come to another dimension in this matter of criticism. Spiritual maturity involves not only the ability to take criticism, but it also involves the ability to give it properly. Solomon stated this concept with total accuracy. *"Faithful are the wounds of a friend,"* **Proverbs 27:6**. This word *"faithful"* is translated from the Hebrew word <u>Aman</u> (aw-man'). <u>Aman</u> is a root word which means to build up or support; to foster as a parent or nurse. [1] Figuratively it means to render (or be) firm or faithful. It is closely akin to another Hebrew word which is spelled and pronounced the same. It means to take the right hand road, to turn to the right.[2] Solomon's message is that whatever words a true friend offers will be designed to help; not hurt: to buildup; not tear down. Criticism must never be given destructively.

CORRECTION IS A PART OF CHRISTIAN RESPOSIBILITY

Before too much talk about how to properly give criticism, attention should be given to whether or not it should be attempted. After all, there is a big risk that you'll make an enemy. People are generally too immature to want their weaknesses exposed, and too lazy to do very much to correct them. In most cases you will be accused of meddling in something that is *none of your business.* You will quite likely be called a self-righteous judge and be told that the Bible says you should not judge. You can be pretty sure that the effort will be to shift the spotlight off the flaw(s) of the person you address and on to you. It is not difficult to see why so few people make efforts to help a friend directly and openly; usually when anything is said, it is behind the back of the person who needs help. That is not a good reflection upon Christianity. Rather than build up one another, too often fear keeps us standing by while a loved one, friend or other needy person in our life goes down, down, down.

At this point it would be good to let God simply speak for Himself on this subject. *"Brethren, if a man be overtaken in a fault, ye which are spiritual, restore such an one in the spirit of meekness; considering thyself, lest thou also be tempted. Bear ye one another's burdens, and so fulfil the law of Christ,"* **Galatians 6:1-2**. This is not a suggestion; it's a command; and it doesn't take a genius to figure out what it means. *"We then that are strong ought to bear the infirmities of the weak, and not to please ourselves. Let every one of us please his neighbour for his good to edification,"* **Romans 15:1-2**. Keep in mind that God does not repeat Himself because He forgot. Among other things, repetition by God speaks of extraordinary importance. *"Now we exhort you, brethren, warn them that are unruly, comfort the feebleminded, support the weak, be patient toward all men,"* **1 Thessalonians 5:14**.

Listen to James. *"Brethren, if any of you do err from the truth, and one convert him; Let him know, that he which converteth the sinner from the error of his way shall save a soul from death, and shall hide a multitude of sins,"* **James 5:19-20**. Pastors are especially commanded to *"Preach the word; be instant in season, out of season; reprove, rebuke, exhort with all longsuffering and doctrine,"* **2 Timothy 4:2**. No command could ever be stronger or more binding than one by Jesus Christ. Here is one of the things He said on the subject of giving criticism. *"Moreover if thy brother shall trespass against thee, go and tell him his fault between thee and him alone: if he shall hear thee, thou hast gained thy brother,"* **Matthew 18:15**.

In our world, even *among* Christians there is a serious absence of this teaching and its practice. I must admit my own weakness in this area. Many times when I knew it was greatly needed I have been afraid to constructively criticize a brother or sister. I've been afraid he would get mad, and that I'd lose a friend. I've been afraid he would misunderstand and think I perceived myself to be perfect or better than him. I've worried that he would misunderstand my intentions and question my motives. I've been afraid he'd think I was trying to boss and run his life, and he's think that I'm a *"know-it-all."* I've feared that I would fail to make myself clear and show my love. I've especially been afraid that he would become my enemy, and *"badmouth"* me to others when I would not be there to explain myself. I've feared that I might discourage him and make him think he's a failure, and that I might even kill his will to try.

I know fear is not of the Lord, but I'm admitting to you that many a time I've withheld criticism from people I love very much and wanted to help because I honestly was afraid. I suspect I am not alone in these fears. These fears are not altogether unfounded. On occasions I have tried to help; and I have lost some friends and made some enemies in the process. You might say I'm a little *"gun-shy."* I've looked down the business end of a few shotguns and have taken a few blasts. Yet, the Scriptures keep haunting me. If I don't do what He says, how can I answer God? How can I get around all those commands about helping brothers and sisters with debilitating spiritual problems? We all know the answer to that; we can't get around those Scriptures. In spite of the high risks involved in helping needy brothers and sisters (many of whom do not even know they're needy), we must do it. We can't rush in like a *bull in a China closet*; there's a right time and place, but we can't ignore the need.

We all claim to be Christians and love the brethren. We're to love sinners whether or not they are brethren. What kind of friend is he, who sees a brother or sister with a life-destroying flaw that is bringing him untold misery and scorn; and yet will not offer a constructive word to help? There is something fundamentally and morally wrong with any of us who will not try to help one we love who is in critical need. That runs counter to the Christian ethic. Yet, it is happening among us all of the time. Take almost any believer among us including preachers. Almost every one of us knows exactly what his or her major flaws are. We've known for years that they had them, and we've discussed those flaws among ourselves; but do you suppose that many of us have ever gone to that one personally, face to face, to offer constructive criticism? Do we lift a hand or open our mouths so that he might see and overcome that weakness or flaw that is sapping his strength? No. We're afraid!

I say to you that there comes a time when a real, true friend will risk anger, getting hurt, being misunderstood, and everything else to rescue a brother who is perishing. Let me add that such help should not be offered for the brother's sake alone; it should also be offered for the sake of the work of God. A brother who continues in an uncorrected flaw does a great deal of harm. He not only hurts himself, he hurts lots of people around him: his family, his church, the general reputation of the cause of Christ. For example, a preacher with a certain type problem can tear up a church. After the carnage and train wreck he can claim that *God called me to another church*. Look out next church! Word gets around; and because of him people get down on preachers and churches and Christianity. Bystanders become disillusioned when they see

Christians take no initiative to correct obvious problems their own ranks. The result is hurt, injury and loss to the work of our God.

Diseases among us must be corrected; not ignored and neglected. Cruelty no; facing reality and taking initiative yes! Failure to correct and control unchristian trends among us spread these trends. Failure generates failure: laziness, a welfare mentality, acceptance of unchristian values, a lack of discipline, weakened attitudes about marriage and the home and this list could go on for a long time. It is still true that *"a little leaven leaveneth the whole lump,"* **Galatians 5:9**.

Several years ago there was a fairly large herd of Rocky Mountain Bighorn sheep on Bristol Head Mountain between Creede and Lake City, Colorado. One got a lung parasite; then another, then another. The whole herd died. (Another herd has been replanted.) Wildlife survives on *the survival of the fittest* principle. The diseased and weak must be corrected or go. Failure can mean the death of the whole herd. Believers must not be cruel and merciless like animals, but they do have an obligation to preserve, protect, and build up the kingdom's work. Love, kindness, understanding and help must be manifested, but the work demands that corrections be made.

CRITICISM THAT HELPS

Before going any farther I want to assure you that I do not have the final word or claim to be an expert on this subject. I do have lots of experience and I also know that what I am about to offer is sound advice from the Word of God. I speak as just one of the troops down in the trenches who sees a grave need; and who would love to help us all do a better job in doing what God has told us to do. It is with this spirit that I offer the following eight considerations on the issue of offering criticism.

Learn to Take Criticism Before You Attempt to Give It

If you attempt to criticize someone who knows you can't take criticism, he will most likely view you as a hypocrite. If he has seen you properly receive it and he knows the process is working in you, then he's much more likely to give ear to what you say.

The Bible is quite clear on this matter. *"Therefore thou art inexcusable, O man, whosoever thou art that judgest: for wherein thou judgest another, thou condemnest thyself; for thou that judgest doest the same things,"* **Romans 2:1**. Jesus personally addressed the issue. *"And why beholdest thou the mote that is in thy brother's eye, but considerest not the beam that is in thine own eye? Or how wilt thou say to thy brother, Let me pull out the mote out of thine eye; and, behold, a beam is in thine own eye? Thou hypocrite, first cast out the beam out of thine own eye; and then shalt thou see clearly to cast out the mote out of thy brother's eye,"* **Matthew 7:3-5**. These verses are saying you must be employing in your life the same process of accepting criticism which you expect your hearer to employ in his. You must have dealt in your own life with the measure which you are attempting to correct in his.

Before you get too bold and start correcting others, spend some time learning how to be corrected. Until you do, your efforts at correcting others will do more harm than good.

Offer Criticism Only As a Friend, Never As a Foe

Solomon said, *"Iron sharpeneth iron; so a man sharpeneth the countenance of his friend,"* **Proverbs 27:17**. The one you attempt to correct must quickly perceive that you are a friend there to help. He must not perceive you as someone intent on beating up on him or that you are there to put him down. He must see that you have no ulterior motive or hypocrisy. He should see in you the heart of a friend and servant, a brokenness and humility. The Bible says, *"By love serve one another,"* **Galatians 5:13**.

In an effort like this you can seriously hurt someone and create bitterness in him that could well send him away permanently on a bad path. God forbid! Jesus warned, *"But whoso shall offend one of these little ones which believe in me, it were better for him that a millstone were hanged about his neck, and that he were drowned in the depth of the sea,"* **Matthew 18:6**. Beware lest you sit on a *holier-than-thou* pedestal, be harsh and cruel, roughshod and unkind and allow yourself to be cavalier.

You will be amazed at how much a brother will accept, if he knows you are really trying to help him: that your motives are sparkling pure, that you are as a friend in the same foxhole, not an adversary.

Offer Criticism Only in Humility and Meekness

You cannot offer reproof or criticism in a spirit of superiority and arrogance, and expect it to be favorably received. The Apostle Peter wrote, *"Yea, all of you be subject one to another, and be clothed with humility: for God resisteth the proud, and giveth grace to the humble,"* **1 Peter 5:5**. Yes, God *resists the proud* and so do most people. If you attempt to criticize someone in pride and arrogance, you will make matters worse instead of better. That eliminates offering criticism out of anger.

Go in humility and meekness making no claim to extra holiness or greatness. You are functioning simply as one child of God to another child of God: one needy sinner to another.

Paul was absolutely explicit on this point, *"Brethren, if a man be overtaken in a fault, ye which are spiritual, restore such an one in the spirit of meekness: considering thyself, lest thou also be tempted."* **Galatians 6:1**. A *"spirit of meekness"* is vital. This is not saying that you are to be weak and vacillating. No. Be firm and sure; but act and speak humbly. Disobey this and you will surely fail.

Offer Criticism Only From a Sensitive Heart of Love

The Apostle Paul told us to *"walk worthy of the vocation wherewith ye are called, With all lowliness and meekness, with longsuffering, forbearing one another in love; Endeavouring to keep the unity of the Spirit in the bond of peace,"* **Ephesians 4:1-3**. If we do this, we will always be sensitive to the person's need and to their capacity to handle the criticism. Love *"is kind,"* **1 Corinthians 13:4**, and feels the anguish of a friend.

Sometimes people are just not ready to hear all they need to hear. They are newborns in the family of God. Even older Christians may have been hurt or disillusioned by some Christian. They are very low and discouraged. Too much strong medicine could be more than they're ready to take. Generally you have to wait for an opening, the right moment. To force yourself into the picture when the time is not right can close the door permanently in your face. That's especially true where a marriage is in trouble. Sometimes during the process of a session to help someone tempers start to rise. When that happens it's usually best to back off. Mr. Counselor, your spirit must be ever sensitive. You should not attempt the critique until the time is right.

Oh how beautiful the words of this key verse! *"Faithful are the wounds of a friend,"* **Proverbs 27:6**. Like a nursemaid the true critic is always loving, tender and caring. The Apostle Paul could be terse, but he wrote to the Thessalonians, *"But we were gentle among you, even as a nurse cherisheth her children,"* **1 Thessalonians 2:7**. May that be our heart and approach toward all we would help! Understanding, mercy, gentleness and kindness must be our approach and practice. That applies to everyone including your mate and other family members. Sometimes we forget that and take them for granted.

Offer Only Valid Criticism

Don't open your mouth until you know what you're talking about and can prove it to your friend. That means before you ever bring up the issue to your brother, you must examine the situation very carefully to be certain you are not misreading it. That takes time, but you must be on target when you speak; and be able to show your friend the validity of what you say. At first he probably won't see. He is likely to become a bit angry, resist and attempt to deny it and/or excuse himself. It is common for people when affronted with a weakness or sin to turn the spotlight; probably on you or on some other person. It will take considerable proof by you to open his eyes. You will not succeed with blanket accusations; you will need specific examples and incidents that justify and make the case.

It is not difficult to see why wise Solomon said, *"The heart of the righteous studieth to answer,"* **Proverbs 15:28**. Get your facts together and structure them in sufficient order to make your case. You have to know what you're talking about in order to make your case. Otherwise you will never succeed. It is the truth that opens the eyes, **John 8:32**. If your friend knows you're telling him the truth, he is likely to stay tuned; but once he decides you really don't know what you're talking about, he's likely to resent you for even attempting to talk to him.

Offer Your Criticism Clearly and Without Ambiguity

My, it's easy to *"beat around the bush"* especially when you are nervous and afraid that you are going to say the wrong thing. Sometimes we are so vague that those we would help miss the whole point. Paul spoke of clear words, easy to be understood. He said, *"For if the trumpet give an uncertain sound, who shall prepare himself to the battle? So likewise ye, except ye utter by the tongue words easy to be understood, how shall it be known what is spoken? for ye shall speak into the air,"* **1 Corinthians 14:8-9**.

Don't confuse those you would help. Be gentle and kind; but be frank, firm, and clear. Don't skirt the issue(s). Get to the point and help the person understand, *see it.* Don't leave the person dangling, uncertain and confused. Use words that are concise and explicit. Job said, *"Teach me, and I will hold my tongue: and cause me to understand wherein I have erred. How forcible are right words! but what doth your arguing reprove?"* **Job 6:24-25**.

Offer Your Criticism to Your Brother's Face, Not Behind His Back

It is a sad commentary on Christianity that most of us are verbose and pointed in our criticism. We are experts on everybody's flaws and problems, and we psychoanalyze them regularly. The big problem is that we do it behind their backs; seldom to their faces. Much of it gets back to the ones we criticize; but when it does, it is distorted, twisted and void of love and understanding. The results are disastrous: broken relationships, resentments, anger, betrayal, misunderstandings, counterattacks and untold injury to God's people and work.

How out of sync this practice is with Jesus who said, *"Moreover if thy brother shall trespass against thee, go and tell him his fault between thee and him alone: if he shall hear thee, thou hast gained thy brother,"* **Matthew 18:15**! Solomon explained the right way to do it. *"Debate thy cause with thy neighbor himself; and discover not a secret to another,"* **Proverbs 25:9**.

In your whole life, how many people have ever sought you out privately and in a spirit of meekness and humility to help you see one of your problems? How many have you sought out and helped in this godly fashion? The practice is rare, far too rare!

Be Willing to Help the Brother Who Is In Need of Correction

Enabling a brother to see his need is a big help; but it's a bigger help when you roll up your sleeves and get in there to work with him to cure the problem. James said that merely telling a brother to be warmed and clothed is not enough. Listen to his heart-piercing words. *"If a brother or sister be naked, and destitute of daily food, And one of you say unto them, Depart in peace, be ye warmed and filled; notwithstanding ye give them not those things which are needful to the body; what doth it profit?"* **James 2:15-16**. People in need of change must often have more than words; they must have follow-through. Sometimes you have to go back, spend time and show lots of continuing love and concern. This is the true face of unselfishness and giving. Jesus said, *"It is more blessed to give than to receive,"* **Acts 20:35**. What better way is there to invest your life than to serve God by helping others?

You'll be surprised at how much criticism a brother will accept, if it is offered right. Not all, but some people will come to love, appreciate and respect you for it. No wonder Jesus said, *"Give, and it shall be given unto you; good measure, pressed down, and shaken together, and running over, shall men give into your bosom. For with the same measure that ye mete withal it shall be measured to you again,"* **Luke 6:38**.

"FAITHFUL ARE THE WOUNDS OF A FRIEND"

Almost always criticism hurts. Those who receive it feel wounded; however, wounds are not always bad. Like a doctor who makes an incision to remove a cancer, a wound can be a welcome prospect and we can be thankful for it. No, we don't like the diagnosis of a tumor, and the removal is painful; but it's worth it. The end result is good. We know we've been delivered from a problem that left unchecked could have resulted in much agony to us personally as well as those around us, and it could have put us in an early grave. Let us thank God for faithful friends who love us enough to risk our ire, scorn and rejection to tell us the truth about ourselves.

THERE IS MORE TO COME ON THIS SUBJECT

We are looking at maturity. We're considering behavior that speaks of its presence, and the absence of which speaks of immaturity. The probe is not over. We must also look at adversity: trials such as sickness, job loss, major accidents and even the death of a dear loved one. More often than any other factor in life, adversity separates the men from the boys. The next few chapters in this book will explore the issue of adversity as a measure of Christian maturity.

---

[1] James Strong, *Greek Dictionary of the New Testament,* (Nashville, Tennessee: Abingdon Press, 1958), reference 539.

[2] Ibid., reference 541.

Chapter 11

Response to Adversity

MAJOR TESTING

Adversity! Webster calls it "misfortune; bad luck; poverty and trouble."[1] Something *adverse* to you means it is against or opposed to you. Adversity is commonly viewed as harmful, not helpful.[2] The Bible word is *"afflict"* or *"afflicted."* Actually there are two Hebrew words with identical spelling and pronunciation, but their meanings are not the same. The words are anah'; they are sometimes mistakenly interchanged. One of these words carries the idea of looking down or browbeating.[3]

Who wants adversity, trouble and affliction? Not very many! We know the Israeli story of servitude in Egyptian bondage, and how it left an indelible and lasting impression on them and on the entire world. *"The Egyptians evil entreated us, and afflicted us, and laid upon us hard bondage,"* **Deuteronomy 26:6**. While the Exodus is a classic story of freedom, it is also a story of oppression, deep suffering and anguish. For most of us, the prospect of adversity and suffering runs a cold chill down our spine. *Lord, I want to be a really good Christian and I want you to use me to great advantage to your cause, but I don't want any trouble.*

The fact is that trouble and adversity will test your mettle and reveal who you really are in an unparalleled way. There is no exam like the refiner's fire to check the quality of your silver,

Zechariah 13:9, and no process like trial by fire to purify your gold, **Job 23:10**. Friend, we're about to look at you. Christian, please don't use this lens to evaluate someone around you; use it to evaluate you. How mature are you? Your response to adversity is a measuring device that will tell you much about your growth level.

A WORD ABOUT ADVERSITY

Job found himself nose deep in adversity. Like *"good Christians"* of most ages, his *friends* accredited his adversity to deep, hidden sin in his life. *"Remember, I pray thee, who ever perished, being innocent? or where were the righteous cut off? Even as I have seen, they that plow iniquity, and sow wickedness, reap the same,"* **Job 4:7-8**. *Job, your adversity is a direct result of sin in your life.* A few hundred years later a group of religious elitists' asked Jesus a loaded question which reflected their preconceived belief that one's troubles are a direct result of sin in one's life. *"And as Jesus passed by, he saw a man which was blind from his birth. And his disciples asked him, saying, Master, who did sin, this man, or his parents, that he was born blind?"* **John 9:1-2**. Surely, they thought, this blind man's condition is a result of either his sin or sin in his parents. Sometimes people do face adverse punishment as a direct result of specific sin in their lives (*"sin, when it is finished, bringeth forth death,"* **James 1:15**), but immediate sin is not always the cause of adversity. Jesus answered the clueless *experts*, *"Neither hath this man sinned, nor his parents: but that the works of God should be made manifest in him. I must work the works of him that sent me,"* **John 9:3-4**. There was another reason for this man's adversity; Jesus was about to use him as an object lesson. He was going to show and demonstrate His power and glory in this man. Not always, but sometimes it's that way. God chooses a man or woman for special service. In this person He will demonstrate His power. In the deepest of valleys He will sustain this person. He will give the strength, the courage, the good spirit and all else it takes for this person to showcase real, biblical Christianity. The person may suffer with a beautiful spirit and testimony in spite of adversity. He may come out on the other side of the valley stronger and better than ever. Job did. He may die with grace. Paul did.

No. Not all adversity is punishment for sin. God has other purposes.

An Important Component in a Much Greater Enterprise

The work of God is infinitely greater than any one individual. The Bible makes clear that His primary eternal purpose is glory to His self. A big part of that purpose is the redemption of fallen man. All that He is doing at any given moment is beyond the ability of human comprehension. *"O the depth of the riches both of the wisdom and knowledge of God! how unsearchable are his judgments, and his ways past finding out!"* **Romans 11:33**. In any given church there are high profile and low profile members, yet the church is *"one body,"* **1 Corinthians 12:20**. Likewise, the work of God is of world-wide scope and involves multitudes of people over many centuries. Even high profile Christians appear on God's big stage for only brief appearances. Whether high or low profile, it is the job of every Christian to glorify God in one way or another. One may be a great preacher or Christian leader, another may be an unknown servant serving far below the radar, but each has a purpose in the whole. Fannie Crosby wrote great hymns, Charles Spurgeon preached home-run sermons to multitudes and James Strong gave us a phenomenal tool called a concordance along with Hebrew and Greek dictionaries complete with indexing. For every Crosby, Spurgeon and Strong, there are untold millions of unnamed servants who laid it all on the line for the cause of Christ. *"And what shall I more say? for the time would fail me to tell of Gedeon, and of Barak, and of Samson, and of Jephthae; of David also, and Samuel, and of the prophets: Who through faith subdued kingdoms, wrought righteousness, obtained promises, stopped the mouths of lions, Quenched the violence of fire, escaped the edge of the sword, out of weakness were made strong, waxed valiant in fight, turned to flight the armies of the aliens. Women received their dead raised to life again: and others were tortured, not accepting deliverance; that they might obtain a better resurrection: And others* *had trial of cruel mockings and scourgings, yea, moreover of bonds and imprisonment: They were stoned, they were sawn asunder, were tempted, were slain with the sword: they wandered about in sheepskins and goatskins; being destitute, afflicted, tormented; (Of whom the world was not worthy:) they wandered in deserts, and in mountains, and in dens and caves of the earth. And these all, having obtained a good report through faith, received not the promise,"* **Hebrews 11:32-39**.

God gets glory for Himself in many ways. Sometimes it's upfront and glamourous; sometimes it's not. Glory for Him may come through faithfulness to God when facing a martyr's death, but it may come through faithfulness to God while dying with cancer. Yes, godly responses and attitudes even when your mate dies, your pastor turns corrupt, a *"Christian"* sexually molests you or your child, when you lose your fortune and all you have or when you are old, sick, poor and all alone! Fellow Christian, like Job right now you may be serving a purpose unknown to you, a purpose in the grand scheme of things that is far bigger than you suspect. Your faithfulness to God in the face of your adversity is a testimony to Him. It says the grace of God is real and that it works in the time of need. What He is doing through you may very well be a seed planted in the heart of your child, grandchild or other bystander that will sprout and yield great fruit long after you are dead and gone.

There are many parts in a car. The average driver is unaware of most of them, and if he saw some of them, he wouldn't have a clue as to what they are or their purposes. Just the parts in an automatic transmission will boggle the average mind. They may seem mundane and unimportant, but they're not. Without those O-rings and clutches, those little pumps and capacitors, that nasty ole oil and a whole lot more, that nice machine that you call a car won't run. The Bible says, *"What God hath cleansed, that call not thou common,"* **Acts 10:15**. Fellow-laborer, do not write off yourself. When adversity comes your way, keep in mind that God may be using you in a unique way as an important component in His great enterprise.

A Strengthening and Equipping Process

Most of us know the connection between the beautiful Monarch butterfly and the cocoon in which he grows to maturity. Breaking out of that cocoon is an arduous undertaking; the butterfly can barely do it. He must strain and push and give every ounce of his strength to the process. It seems too much, too painful and too hard; but oddly enough it is that process which enables the butterfly to fly. All that straining and pushing strengthens the butterfly, otherwise he is doomed to perish. Well-meaning bystanders have helped butterflies prematurely break free. Invariably they die unable to fly.

God uses adversity to strengthen us. It is a primary tool in stimulating our growth. We generally do not like it, and sometimes we moan, complain and react in really childish ways; but adversity handled in the Christian way helps us. You've probably noticed that the strongest, wisest, most courageous and most consistent Christians are not the young ones who are mostly *mouth* and sometimes full of passion and zeal without knowledge. No. They're the ones who have fought lots of battles, been through lots of fire and faced enormous trials and adversity. Somehow the rough road tempered and strengthened them. It gave them wisdom beyond themselves. You decided that in case of a dog-fight, you wanted to be in the foxhole with this person.

Yes. Adversity teaches us. It breaks through the crust and gets down to reality. It enables us to endure with patience and make better judgments. It teaches us the difference between glitter and gold. The man whom God used to write Psalm 119 said, *"Before I was afflicted I went astray: but now have I kept thy word,"* **Psalm 119:67**. *"Before I was afflicted"* I went astray; but afterwards I did better. Affliction helped me. As painful as it was, I am thankful that God afflicted me, brought me into circumstances that were hard to take. I needed that and it was good for me. *"It is good for me that I have been afflicted; that I might learn thy statutes,"* **Psalm 119:71**. Oh, how nice it would be to develop big and strong muscles without the sweat and toil of exercise, but that is not how it works. The ones who are able to best help us with our pain and grief are the ones who've known pain and grief. The experts in patience are those who've endured long hardships. The ones who know the Scriptures and how to apply them are the ones who've labored and labored and labored in the Word and in the lives of others. There are no magic shortcuts. We cannot legitimately expect to bypass adversity and still be seasoned in the work of God. Hard times are a part of the strengthening process.

The Apostle Paul knew plenty about adversity. Often he asked God to deliver him from some of the adversity he faced. In one case Paul asked God three times to take away a problem. God didn't deliver him from that problem, but He did give Paul the help he needed to endure. *"For this thing I besought the Lord thrice, that it might depart from me. And he said unto me, My grace is sufficient for thee: for my strength is made perfect in weakness,"* **2 Corinthians 12:8-9**. In view of what God could use adversity to do to and through him, Paul concluded, *"Most gladly therefore will I rather glory in my infirmities, that the power of Christ may rest upon me. Therefore I take pleasure in infirmities, in reproaches, in necessities, in persecutions, in distresses for Christ's sake: for when I am weak, then am I strong,"* **2 Corinthians 12:9-10**. Oh that all of us who know the Blessed Redeemer would realize that He is always seeking to grow and strengthen us, even when conditions are adverse! *"All things,"* not just the pleasant, stress-less ones, really do *"work together for good to them that love God, to them who are the called according to his purpose,"* **Romans 8:28**. When adversity enters your life keep in mind that God may be strengthening a weakness in you. He may be preparing you (getting you ready) for a major event that is heading your way, an event that will take every ounce of strength you have.

An Object Lesson by God

God may also be using you as a divine object lesson. God is a teacher that commonly uses object lessons in the Scriptures. Repeatedly throughout the ages God has used a person or physical object to teach and illustrate some spiritual truth. He used Pharaoh to show what it's like to harden yourself against God, a brass serpent to show that salvation is by grace through faith and the nation of Israel to illustrate His dealings with His people. Jesus used a little child to teach the need for innocence, simplicity and faith in grown people, **Matthew 18:2-5**.

Sometimes God uses a specific person in which to showcase His power. We Christians are pretty bold about our claims that God's grace is sufficient to meet all needs. We quote passages like *"My grace is sufficient for thee: for my strength is made perfect in weakness,"* **2 Corinthians 12:9** and *"There hath no temptation taken you but such as is common to man: but God is faithful, who will not suffer you to be tempted above that ye are able; but will with the temptation also make a way to escape, that ye may be able to bear it,"* **1 Corinthians 10:13.** Oh really? The world around us wants to *see* (yes *see*) God's grace. Somebody needs to back up this high and lofty rhetoric. They need a case in point. Your kids need to see it. Your neighbors need to see it. People where you work need to see it. People at your church need to see it. Most of them have only seen pious Christians talk about how great God is and how He helps and sustains His own, but when adversity came (major sickness, financial woes, a disastrous wreck or fire, catastrophe), the bold talk evaporated like a morning fog. What they *saw* in those "pious Christians" was dejection, complaining, criticism of and disillusionment with God and abandonment of Christianity. *Why me, God? This is not fair. I've served you all this time and now you've deserted me. I quit church, all that holy stuff and this religion thing.* Yes, that's what the world has *seen* in too many Christians. Oh what a need there is for people like Job, Christians who are real, not mere fair-weather pretenders! There's a need for object lessons, for people/examples in which God can showcase the validity of His claims.

GOD MAY USE YOU AS AN OBJECT LESSON

How God goes about choosing specific people remains a mystery, but sometimes one person becomes His showcase. It is clear from the cases of Job, Paul and the blind man of **John 9** that the chosen person is not there because of deep, dark sin in his life or because of poor choices or blundering mismanagement. To the contrary, these people constitute the elite of God. They are chosen for one of the hardest of God's jobs, to do what most others could not handle. If God allows you the opportunity to suffer for Him in a unique way of adversity where few ever serve, don't despair and complain. Shine! Let people see His power to comfort, sustain and meet every need in you. Let them see a good spirit, full submission and a deepening love and appreciation for God in you. Remember what the Apostle Paul said, *"Ye are our epistle written in our hearts, known and read of all men: Forasmuch as ye are manifestly declared to be the epistle of Christ ministered by us, written not with ink, but with the Spirit of the living God; not in tables of stone, but in fleshy tables of the heart,"* **2 Corinthians 3:2-3**. People are watching. They're watching *you.* Your mate is watching. Your children are watching. They're watching at work and at church. The vast majority of the world's people never read a Bible; they read you. Their idea of God and Christianity comes from you. *Is this Christianity real? Does it really work? It is all rhetoric? Is there any real substance to it?* Christian, if God puts you in the spotlight, don't blow it!

HOW IT WORKS

The Bible is loaded with great promises for God's people. *"I can do all things through Christ which strengtheneth me,"* **Philippians 4:13**. *"But my God shall supply all your need according to his riches in glory by Christ Jesus,"* **Philippians 4:19**. *"I will never leave thee, nor forsake thee,"* **Hebrews 13:5**. Jesus said, *"Peace I leave with you, my peace I give unto you: not as the world giveth, give I unto you. Let not your heart be troubled, neither let it be afraid"* **John 14:27**. The Apostle Paul called it *"the peace of God, which passeth all understanding,"* **Philippians 4:7**. The Bible is loaded with others. We claim courage, inner strength, peace and rejoicing even in the teeth of life's greatest adversities. We brag about God's grace to save from sin's penalty, to sustain in the hour of need and to ultimately deliver us into the presence of God. We say His grace applies to all who know Him as Savior and Lord.

Our God knows these things and occasionally sets forth to prove one or more of His claims in a real, live test case. He allows a situation in one of His children where special help is needed, an adverse situation. Suddenly the demonstration is on.

TWO POSSIBILITIES

A favorable outcome is not guaranteed. God's child may or may not cooperate. Too many resist God's efforts to showcase His power in them. As previously indicated, they turn sour and bitter toward God. Instead of allowing God to work through them to demonstrate His power and promises, they react negatively toward their adversity and behave as if the claims of the Bible are lies. It is not difficult to see what happens when loud-talking Christians crack as soon as they are put on display under stress.

There are those who allow God to use them to the fullest. Bystanders see courage, peace and submission. They see the hurt and merciless adversity, yet there is no resentment, anger, bitterness, fighting and critical spirit. There is no self-pity and second-guessing of God. Instead there is praise and a beautiful spirit. The sustaining grace and goodness of God are highlighted, there is hope and bystanders can *see* that the claims of God are real. In this person bystanders see a live demonstration of that which they read in the Bible and heard at church.

YOUR BEST OPPORTUNITY TO REALLY SHINE FOR GOD

You may think you can see farthest at noonday when sunlight is at its zenith. That is not the case. You can actually see farthest on the darkest night. That is when you see millions upon millions of stars many of which are light-years away. At noon the only star you can see is the sun. Believer, you are never shining brighter for the Lord than when the situation around you is darkest. Anyone can talk a good show. *Fair-weather Christians* are *a dime a dozen.* The champion is the one who steps up and shines even in the face of life's toughest adversity. He's the one who distinguishes himself in the fiercest and bitterest of life's storms and battles. Our nation does not give the *Red Badge of Courage* to one who never went to battle or a *Purple Heart* to one who never sustained a wound. We don't award the *Congressional Medal of Honor* to the professors at West Point or the Air Force Academy. No! The laurels go to the men who were there, in the trenches, on the front lines where the suffering and dying was. Honor goes to those who faced adversity. The greater the test, the higher the honor.

Christian brother/sister, as you honor God and give your best in some lonely trench, do not despair. If God has chosen you to be a *Green Beret* or a *Navy Seal,* let Him make a star out of you. One day all of God's soldiers of the cross will stand before God. *"Every man's work shall be made manifest: for the day shall declare it, because it shall be revealed by fire; and the fire shall try every man's work of what sort it is. If any man's work abide which he hath built thereupon, he shall receive a reward,"* **1 Corinthians 3:13-14**. Some of the great champions of God throughout the ages will step to the platform. There, in full view of the multitudes of heaven, the omnipotent King of kings and Lord of lords will say, *"Well done, thou good and faithful servant,"* **Matthew 25:21**. By His own hand He will crown them with glory that will never fade away. *"And when the chief Shepherd shall appear, ye shall receive a crown of glory that fadeth not away,"* **1 Peter 5:4**. It is not difficult to see why the Apostle Paul wrote, *"For I reckon that the sufferings of this present time are not worthy to be compared with the glory which shall be revealed in us,"* **Romans 8:18**.

Who will they be? No doubt on that day we are going to see who the real heroes and champions of the faith are. Many of them will not be who you might expect, like the glamor people who put on big shows and tooted their own horns. Instead they will be the ones who stood firm when the storm was raging, those whose lives shined for God even when the world and their own diseased and time wrecked bodies were caving in around them. They'll be the ones who didn't turn sour and dishonor God by anything they said or did even when the pressure was enormous and cruel.

A WAY FOR YOU TO MEASURE YOU

Your response to adversity is a way for you to measure your own Christian maturity. To some degree this chapter is about practicing what you preach. You can know lots of Scripture, be quite pious, become passionate and animated in your worship and service, toot your own horn, be addicted to and deeply involved in your church and be most sincere; but until you start living your Christianity even in hard times, there is no serious maturity.

Response to adversity is a true spiritual measuring device. It is the people who stand true and faithful even in the midst of the storms who have grown up in the Lord.

THERE IS MORE

Any discussion about marks of Christian maturity would be incomplete without a look at spiritual reproduction. The next chapter of this book will examine this obvious marker.

---

1 *Webster's New World Dictionary with Student Handbook: Young People's Edition*, s.v. "adversity," (Nashville, Tennessee: The World Publishing Company, 1973), 12.

2 *Webster's*, s.v. "adverse."

3 James Strong, *Hebrew and Chaldee Dictionary,* (Nashville, Tennessee: Abingdon Press, 1958), reference 6031.

Chapter 12

Spiritual Reproduction

As we have moved through the chapters of this book, we have looked at the essence of spiritual maturity: faith, hope, and charity. This is the heart part that only God sees. We have also focused our attention on several outward manifestations of true maturity: fundamental honesty, humility, personal discipline, wisdom, proper response to criticism and proper response to adversity. People see these.

We are about to examine one more manifestation of true spiritual maturity, the practice of reproducing yourself in the lives of others. The consistent bringing of new people into the family of God coupled with the development of the aforementioned qualities in other believers marks a Christian as one who has grown up to full age in the Lord. The Bible speaks of *"them that are of full age, even those who by reason of use have their senses exercised to discern both good and evil,"* **Hebrews 5:14**.

AN OBVIOUS PHENOMENON

Throughout the natural world, reproduction is accepted as a sure sign of sexual maturity and sexual maturity is generally associated with overall maturity. Whales, elephants, finches or fleas are considered mature when they are able to breed. So are people.

We make a distinction between physical, mental and emotional maturity; however, most of the time we don't slice the picture that thin. A person is either mature or immature, and the most decisive earmark is one's ability to reproduce. Barring some sort of pathology, no one can legitimately be considered mature until he attains that capability.

SPIRITUAL REPRODUCTION

Parallels between the natural world and the spiritual world appear repeatedly in the Scriptures. The *"secrets of wisdom"* are mentioned and the claim is made *"that they are double to that which is!"* **Job 11:6**. We have *"fathers of our flesh"* and there is *"the Father of spirits,"* **Hebrews 12:9**. Jesus spoke of a natural birth and a spiritual birth, **John 3:6**. Like Adam and Eve, natural parents produce physical children, **Genesis 4:1-2**, and Christians can produce spiritual children, which is the primary message of Jesus' Great Commission, **Matthew 28:18-20**. Saved people are to (1) bring others to salvation, (2) bring them to a legitimate baptism and (3) help them to grow to maturity in the ways set forth in the Scriptures.

It is not enough to become saved or *born again* and sit on it; God expects you to bring about a *New Birth* in another person. And another! And another! It's not enough to be taught. The *taught* are to *"teach others also,"* **2 Timothy 2:2**. *"Freely ye have received, freely give,"* **Matthew 10:8**. The God of heaven did not give His Son to pay that agonizing price of redemption so that you or I could stagnate like a lake with no outlet. Every good thing that we have received is to be replicated in others.

There are two primary areas of spiritual reproduction.

Bringing Lost People to a Saving Knowledge of Christ

The greatest need of lost people is forgiveness of sins and eternal life, and God's first assignment to saved people is *"Go ye into all the world, and preach the gospel to every creature,"* **Mark 16:15**. The Apostle Paul wrote to the Corinthians, *"For I delivered unto you first of all that which I also received, how that Christ died for our sins according to the scriptures; And that he was buried, and that he rose again the third day according to the scriptures,"* **1 Corinthians 15:3-4**. The death, burial and resurrection of Jesus Christ is the gospel message. It is *"the power of God unto salvation,"* **Romans 1:16**. When men hear and believe this message, their sins are forgiven and they are given eternal life. It's the message Paul heard which resulted in his *New Birth.* The first thing Paul did when he met new people was seek to bring about a spiritual *New Birth* in them. *"I delivered unto you first of all that which I also received."* Every human has the same basic need and there is only one message that can meet that need.

In Paul we see the clear pattern for spiritual reproduction, which is to initially seek to bring about the *New Birth* in others. This was Jesus' approach with Nicodemus, **John 3:1-21**, with the woman at the well, **John 4:5-26**, and with Zaccheus, **Luke 19:1-10**. Bringing others to Christ is spiritual reproduction in the most fundamental sense of the concept. *"He that goeth forth and weepeth, bearing precious seed, shall doubtless come again with rejoicing, bringing his sheaves with him,"* **Psalm 126:6**. Don't go to heaven empty-handed. Take others with you, especially your children, but also your friends and neighbors. Reach out. Get into lives. Tell them about the redemptive work of Jesus Christ. *"How then shall they call on him in whom they have not believed? and how shall they believe in him of whom they have not heard? and how shall they hear without a preacher?"* **Romans 10:14**.

Bringing Saved People to Spiritual Maturity

Reproduction does not end with a baby in a crib. Beyond the delivery room there is work, work, work and untold training to do. A newborn babe doesn't even know how to talk or walk. Babies mostly sleep, eat, cry and need diaper changes.

There is a striking parallel between physical newborns and spiritual newborns. Spiritual newborns need lots of attention too.

They have to be taught and trained. They are *new creatures* in Christ, **2 Corinthians 5:17**, but they still have an old fleshly nature, **Ephesians 4:22**. They do not innately know how to properly behave in a Christian manner. Among other things that means to tell and practice truth, to deal with a temper and fleshly lusts, to return good for evil, to pray or study the Bible, to go to church and properly worship and serve there. They do not know how to apply the truths of God's Word (most of which they've never learned).

A part of spiritual reproduction is helping newborns grow up. It's causing them to learn and apply the truths of God. There is nothing quite like hands-on training to bring about growth. It's being around to observe and instruct. It's being an example and showing *how to* do things. It's correcting mistakes, giving encouragement and being patience with the one who hasn't yet grown up. Boys have to be taught how to be men and girls are not automatically good wives or mothers. Paul showed the Philippians how to behave like the people of God. He provided himself as an example. *"Those things, which ye have both learned, and received, and heard, and seen in me, do,"* **Philippians 4:9**. We need to use this hand's-on training that is designed to reproduce ourselves in the lives of other people.

This kind of reproduction is all over the Scriptures. You see it in Moses who reproduced himself in Joshua, in Elijah and Elisha, in Paul and Timothy and in Jesus and the apostles. A great hindrance to the work of God has been the failure of God's people to reproduce themselves in a next generation. Too many fathers with a strong work ethic didn't reproduce it in their sons. Somehow we didn't reproduce a spirit of giving, a forgiving heart, kindness, compassion, dependability, the assuming of responsibility, thankful and appreciative hearts, loyalty, fidelity, integrity and this list could go on for a very long time.

SPIRITUAL REPRODUCTION IS REALLY BIG WITH GOD

No Scripture says it more succinctly, clearly or forcefully than **2 Timothy 2:2**. *"And the things that thou hast heard of me among many witnesses, the same commit thou to faithful men, who shall be able to teach others also."* Pass it on, pass it on, pass it on just come booming out of this verse. Four generations: (1) Paul to (2) Timothy to (3) *"faithful men"* to (4) *"others."*

God knows human nature. People forget in a hurry, especially from one generation to the next. They will leave God and all for which He stands. *"And the LORD said unto Moses, Behold, thou shalt sleep with thy fathers; and this people will rise up, and go a whoring after the gods of the strangers of the land, whither they go to be among them, and will forsake me, and break my covenant which I have made with them,"* **Deuteronomy 31:16**. The next generation will do it, even your own children and grandchildren. They will turn from the God of the Bible and from His precepts that are given in His Word. They will become tolerant of other gods and lifestyles, and become sympathizers. In a few generations they will throw out the one true God and reject His ways (Christianity). We are currently seeing it happen in America. The only safeguard against this trend is spiritual reproduction in god-fearing people. God knew the constant and insidious power of decadence and instructed Israel (and His people throughout the ages) to reproduce themselves in their children. *"And these words, which I command thee this day, shall be in thine heart: And thou shalt teach them diligently unto thy children, and shalt talk of them when thou sittest in thine house, and when thou walkest by the way, and when thou liest down, and when thou risest up. And thou shalt bind them for a sign upon thine hand, and they shall be as frontlets between thine eyes. And thou shalt write them upon the posts of thy house, and on thy gates,"* **Deuteronomy 6:6-9**.

TWO KINDS OF BABIES

In the first chapter of this book we talked about two kinds of babies: <u>brephos</u> and <u>nepios</u>. <u>Brephos</u> is the Greek word used to speak of a whole, healthy baby or young child. The other word nepios speaks of people who are old enough to show signs of maturity, but who are thinking and behaving like little babies or children. Mentally handicapped people fall into this category; however, Paul used the word in **1 Corinthians 3:1-4** to speak of Christians who are mentally whole, but who think and behave far below their spiritual age.

Obviously it is possible for believers to think and behave far below themselves. There has been ample time for them to grow up, but along the way they stopped developing. They have plenty of time to learn to cooperate and live in constructive harmony and peace, but like little spoiled children they bicker and murmur. They pair-off in little cliques and squabble among themselves. The Corinthian syndrome has survived throughout the ages. The population of nepios is still very high. At the risk of sounding repetitive, I will repeat a Scripture that reflects the thinking of God on this condition. *"Of whom we have many things to say, and hard to be uttered, seeing ye are dull of hearing. For when for the time ye ought to be teachers, ye have need that one teach you again which be the first principles of the oracles of God; and are become such as have need of milk, and not of strong meat. For every one that useth milk is unskilful in the word of righteousness: for he is a babe. But strong meat belongeth to them that are of full age, even those who by reason of use have their senses exercised to discern both good and evil,"* **Hebrews 5:11-14**.

Spiritually immature believers are *"babes"* in the worst sense of the word. After sufficient time for growth, those who do not reproduce true Christianity in the lives of others (both salvation and growth) are immature. They may be pious, know lots of Scripture, be quite busy doing *the work of the Lord*, be passionate and sincere and be able to put on quite a show in a worship service, but they are not mature. The fact that they have reached the potential to reproduce themselves but have not means they are nepios. The ability is there, but the performance is not. After plenty of time there are no spiritual babies, no souls won to Christ and few (if any) fingerprints on the lives of other. What a reproach!

Maturity means reproduction, plain and simple! There can be no skirting this truth. All of the other *good stuff* is quite empty until you start passing real Christianity on to the next generation.

Are you a Christian? How many spiritual children do you have? How many have you brought into the family of God? Upon how many growing Christians can we find your fingerprints? Are you purposefully and actively into the business of reproducing yourself in the lives of others? The first commandment of the Bible (not the second or third) is *"Be fruitful, and multiply,"* **Genesis 1:28**. There is no reason to believe that command (yes, *command*) is limited to physical reproduction. (It initially applies to the physical realm, but it is just as applicable to the spiritual realm.)

A SOBERING REALITY

Apart from reproduction, a whole species or society can vanish in one generation. For your beliefs and values to live beyond your lifetime, you must reproduce yourself in someone who will carry them on once you are gone. The only reason you are here today is because someone reproduced himself in you. Would you like to see real, firs-century, Bible Christianity continue once you are gone? What are you doing to make it happen? Would you like to see strong, godly Christians carry on the great truths and virtues of the Bible? In whom are you investing yourself to guarantee it? If we fail here, there will not be a next generation of our kind.

WE ARE MOVING ON

Christian, look at yourself. Yes, take a long, hard look. How long have you been saved? How would you rate your spiritual maturity? Are you satisfied with where you are? What does the observable evidence say? How do you think God feels about where you are?

For several chapters we have been looking at observable characteristics which speak of true spiritual maturity. Their presence or absence in your life marks you in one way or the other. In the third section of this book we will focus on obstacles to spiritual growth, growth stimulators and other information intended to help you reach your full potential in the Lord.

STIMULATING MATURITY

Chapter 13

Obstacles to Spiritual Growth

Some wise guy said, *"The road to hell is paved with good intentions."* That's probably not the only road that is paved with good intentions. Procrastination is the enemy of all of us. It's easy to be slow about doing something that should be done, to delay something until a later time because it's not easy or convenient to do it now. Deep down there's a lazy streak in most of us.

HEALTHY, WHOLESOME GROWTH

Growth requires much from us. Growth happens naturally; however, for it to be healthy and wholesome, discipline and deliberate effort is required. Bad habits and trends are always vying to get into your picture. As some people grow up, they hang on to *"childish things,"* **1 Corinthians 13:11**. They remain undisciplined. Instead of developing good, balanced eating habits, they make sweets and junk foods their norm. Obesity sets in and often diabetes, cholesterol and other health problems appear at an early age. The childhood propensity to be wild and untamed persists: *I will not be bound by time schedules or deadlines. I will live by my agenda* and *others are not my concern. I will leave my clothes and shoes right where I take them off; for me life is all about fun and games.*

Dependability, responsibility, respect for the property or rights of others and long-range planning are not a part of their psyche. Those *"childish things"* play havoc with jobs, families and most relationships. Growth without discipline and deliberate effort can quickly lead to immorality, bullying, lawlessness, drug addictions, crime and a Pandora's Box of other evils. Furthermore, people can become very good at these things. Yes, it's growth but in a very bad sense.

For healthy, wholesome growth to occur, there must be a deliberate effort. There must be boundaries, rules, *thou shalt* and *thou shalt not*, *these things are acceptable and those are not*! Enforcement and accountability are also in the mix. Civilized societies want their children to grow up with integrity and respect. They realize that healthy, wholesome maturity means honesty, obedience to the law, respect for the feelings and rights of others, self-control, morality and recognition of a supreme being. Without some measure of guidance and deliberate effort, children do not automatically embrace these traits and develop them. King Solomon wisely observed a universal reality, *"The rod and reproof give wisdom: but a child left to himself bringeth his mother to shame,"* **Proverbs 29:15**.

To grow up right, people must have guidance and direction. That is just as true in the spiritual realm as it is in the natural realm. Older, more mature Christians should make it their business to help younger, developing Christians; and younger, developing Christians would do well to recognize their need for the help and wisdom of older, more mature Christians. Mature Christians can steer younger Christians, help them avoid pitfalls and shelter them from dangers. The idea is clearly enunciated in Paul's letter to Titus, *"But speak thou the things which become sound doctrine: That the aged men be sober, grave, temperate, sound in faith, in charity, in patience. The aged women likewise, that they be in behaviour as becometh holiness, not false accusers, not given to much wine, teachers of good things; That they may teach the young women to be sober, to love their husbands, to love their children, To be discreet, chaste, keepers at home, good, obedient to their own husbands, that the word of God be not blasphemed. Young men likewise exhort to be sober minded. In all things shewing thyself a pattern of good works: in doctrine shewing uncorruptness, gravity, sincerity, Sound speech, that cannot be condemned; that he that is of the contrary part may be ashamed, having no evil thing to say of you,"* **Titus 2:1-8**. Note well that *"Aged men"* show the way to *"young men"* and *"aged women"* show the way and teach *"young women."* This is God's pattern for healthy, wholesome spiritual growth to maturity. It's deliberate directed development, not random chance.

BEWARE OF OBSTACLES

As a believer negotiates the road of mortal life, all along the way there will be obstacles, something there to hinder and stop growth. There will be many. Most of them will be subtle, and often they will be cruel. The Apostle Peter spoke specifically of this potential. *"Ye therefore, beloved, seeing ye know these things before, beware lest ye also, being led away with the error of the wicked, fall from your own stedfastness,"* **2 Peter 3:17**. He continued by making it clear that no obstacle should be allowed to stop growth. *"But grow in grace, and in the knowledge of our Lord and Saviour Jesus Christ. To him be glory both now and for ever. Amen,"* **2 Peter 3:18**. Obstacles will come, but they don't have to stop you.

It has been said that *to be forewarned is to be forearmed.* We would all do well to be aware of some of the things that have the potential to stop our spiritual growth.

Satan

Satan is our chief enemy and adversary. *"Be sober, be vigilant; because your adversary the devil, as a roaring lion, walketh about, seeking whom he may devour: whom resist steadfast in the faith, knowing that the same afflictions are accomplished in your brethren that are in the world,"* **1 Peter 5:8-9**. Satan is out to hurt and ruin you. He is neither omniscient, omnipresent nor omnipotent, but he is extremely powerful. Not one of us is a match for him. He is thoroughly evil. He questions and casts doubt on God and His Word, **Genesis 3:1-5**, lies incessantly including to you, **John 8:44**, tempts, **Matthew 4:3**, deceives, **1 Timothy 2:14**, makes evil look good, **2 Corinthians 11:14**, and as Peter said he seeks to destroy you, **1 Peter 5:8**.

Believer, be aware that Satan is always looking for a way to attack you. He wants to bring you down, stop your growth and shipwreck your life. In his letter to young Timothy, the Apostle Paul warned of this danger. He wrote, *"This charge I commit unto thee, son Timothy, according to the prophecies which went before on thee, that thou by them mightest war a good warfare; Holding faith, and a good conscience; which some having put away concerning faith have made shipwreck: Of whom is Hymenaeus and Alexander; whom I have delivered unto Satan, that they may learn not to blaspheme,"* **1 Timothy 1:18-20**. When stumbling-blocks come your way, consider who is at the root of them.

Thank God for the all-powerful Spirit of God who lives in every believer! Through Him we are able to *"resist"* the devil and move forward. Without your voluntary yielding to his devices, Satan cannot stop you. The Apostle John said, *"Ye are of God, little children, and have overcome them: because greater is he that is in you, than he that is in the world,"* **1 John 4:4**. Satan is an adversary and an obstacle to growth, but he cannot stop you against your will. Do not give up and surrender to him. Resist him!

The World and the Flesh

Fleshly appetites and desires do not go away just because a person gets saved. Saved people still live in the same old body and world they were in before they were saved. Jesus pointed out that *"the spirit indeed is willing, but the flesh is weak,"* **Matthew 26:41**. He also said the world is at war with God and the two realms are not in sync, **John 15:18-19**.

The need for food, sex, love, comfort and other fleshly needs is just as great before and after one is saved. It's easy for a new Christian to be drawn back into the old lifestyle that he knew before salvation. When conducted according to the wholesome, liberating principles of true Christianity, there is nothing wrong with meeting the need for food, sex, love, comfort and other fleshly needs. The problem comes when a believer attempts to meet them in ways that leave God out, like gluttony, covetousness, lust, violence, unlawfulness, greed and pride. Peter said, *"Dearly beloved, I beseech you as strangers and pilgrims, abstain from fleshly lusts, which war against the soul,"* **1 Peter 2:11**. Here is how the Apostle Paul put it. *"That ye put off concerning the former conversation the old man,* (the old lifestyle) *which is corrupt according to the deceitful lusts,"* **Ephesians 4:22**. The pull is always there to yield to the flesh and go back to the world's ways which can be attractive. The once productive Demas is a case in point. The Apostle Paul said, *"Demas hath forsaken me, having loved this present world,"* **2 Timothy 4:10**. The flesh and the world are big obstacles to growth and maturity. Yield to them and you will stagnate.

Friends and Family

Those close to you can cause you to stumble. This happens in such a subtle, unsuspecting and unintentional way. Your guard is up against those you don't trust, but it's down when it comes to trusted friends and people you like. They're the ones who will take you out of church to go fishing or play golf. They're the ones who'll show up to visit on a Sunday, but they are not prepared to go to church (and would probably be offended should you go without them). It's often people close to you who discover some new *cure all* health food or water, and who think it should become big to you and that you too should become a crusader for it. There are also the ones who've discovered a revolutionary new eye-popping doctrine or twist on the Scriptures. Most of the time those great new revelations and discoveries will end up undermining you and your faith. This method of derailing good people is not new. In the days when the Bible was being written it was already in use to trip up new believers. Listen to Paul's warning to Titus. *"For there are many unruly and vain talkers and deceivers, specially they of the circumcision: Whose mouths must be stopped, who subvert whole houses, teaching things which they ought not, for filthy lucre's sake,"* **Titus 1:10-11**. Paul said to the Galatians, *"Ye did run well"* and then asked *"who did hinder you that ye should not obey the truth,"* **Galatians 5:7**. *"Hinder you!"* They were growing, progressing in the Lord, becoming mature, but somebody *hindered* them. Be aware that friends and family (and others) can put the brakes on your Christian growth.

Church

The growth of multitudes of Christians has been stopped at church. Yes, really! Of all places church should be a place that stimulates and produces growth, and often it does, but not always. When a church stagnates, most of the people therein stagnate too. Too many times the pastor stagnates and stops growing. He doesn't study enough and consequently stops *feeding the flock,* **Acts 20:28**, solid, meaty sermons. *Reruns* become more frequent, the forward direction of the church slows and sometimes the church goes backward. Everybody stops growing.

Because of the power of the Word of God to produce growth, all members of every church ought to be growing increasingly mature and instability should vanish, but such is not always the case. There was a day when the completed Word of God was not yet finished. During that time God gave *"apostles . . . prophets . . . evangelists and . . . pastors and teachers,"* to build up, edify and unite believers, **Ephesians 4:11**. Shortly thereafter the Scriptures were completed. They are called *"the unity of the faith,"* **Ephesians 4:13**. What is their purpose? To stabilize believers and produce growth in them and in the churches of which they are a part. Listen to the Bible say it. *"Till we all come in the unity of the faith, and of the knowledge of the Son of God, unto a perfect man, unto the measure of the stature of the fulness of Christ: That we henceforth be no more children, tossed to and fro, and carried about with every wind of doctrine, by the sleight of men, and cunning craftiness, whereby they lie in wait to deceive; But speaking the truth in love, may grow up into him in all things, which is the head, even Christ: From whom the whole body fitly joined together and* *compacted by that which every joint supplieth, according to the effectual working in the measure of every part, maketh increase of the body unto the edifying of itself in love,"* **Ephesians 4:13-16**. It's bad to be stuck in a church that serves mostly left-overs and baby food. It's a place where growth to maturity slows or stops. A general survey of modern Christianity, particularly in America, indicates that this condition is widespread in churches.

Churches can also present obstacles to growth in other ways. So many Christians have been hurt and disillusioned in church. Some thoughtless *crack* was made by someone who was supposed to be mature, a scandal broke out right in the church, the church went to civil war and split, the pastor *went off the deep end* and this list could grow quite long. Good people, especially young and immature Christians, get hurt. Their spiritual breath is knocked right out of them. Growth stops and many fall by the wayside and God is mostly left out for the rest of their lives. It's a sad picture, but it's common that Christian *brethren* can stunt or stop the growth of other Christians.

Disappointments and Disillusionments

Only God knows how many good people have fallen due to disappointments and disillusionments. As indicated earlier, it can happen in a church environment; however, disappointments and disillusionments are not limited to churches. I know a young man who moved to a city in a different state. He found himself at a bar. Guess who he saw in the bar? His pastor! He never went back to church. Hypocrisy has enormous power to disillusion. I've heard *Christians* say, *"I don't care what people think."* You'd better care. Jesus said, *"But whoso shall offend one of these little ones which believe in me, it were better for him that a millstone were hanged about his neck, and that he were drowned in the depth of the sea,"* **Matthew 18:6**. Do you know how big a *"millstone"* is? I've watched husbands and wives go to marriage war. They would finger-point and neither would budge. I've also watched what it did to their children (of any age, but especially small children). When it happens, I can't help thinking of that *"millstone."*

What do you suppose happens to the young Christian ladies or young men who are sexually violated by a *friend* who groomed them? How about the employee who is given a raw deal at work? Talk about disappointment and disillusionment! It seems that the greater the expectations, the greater the disappointment and disillusionment when failure occurs. That's especially true when the failure comes at the hands of a professing Christian. The Bible says, *"Fret not thyself because of evildoers,"* **Psalm 37:1**, but people do *"fret."* Many stop growing right there.

Christian, as you move forward in life, be aware that disappointments and disillusionments are the chief tools of Satan to hurt and ruin you. When people fail, keep in mind that it was *"people"* who failed, not God. Keep your eyes on Jesus and your head in His Word. *"Wherefore seeing we also are compassed about with so great a cloud of witnesses, let us lay aside every weight, and the sin which doth so easily beset us, and let us run with patience the race that is set before us, Looking unto Jesus the author and finisher of our faith; who for the joy that was set before him endured the cross, despising the shame, and is set down at the right hand of the throne of God. For consider him that endured such contradiction of sinners against himself, lest ye be wearied and faint in your minds,"* **Hebrews 12:1-3**. Obviously God knows that there is a great propensity to fail or *"faint in your minds"* when people disappoint and hurt you.

Distractions

Many years ago I met a dear man. He was extremely bright, personable and very competent; however, distractions became his downfall. He couldn't stay focused long enough to complete most of his assignments. His *good-heartedness* was a big part of his problem. He wanted to be all things to all people all of the time. He saw needs and he couldn't say *"No."* While on one assignment, some important thing would catch his attention and he'd stop long enough to attend that need. But, as you probably guessed, he'd often be interrupted before he completed that second task. The unconquered propensity ruined this good Christian man. I still know him and it wrecked his life.

In some parts of America the hunting Raccoons is a big sport. A good *coon dog* is worth lots of money, but in order to be a good *coon dog,* the dog must be able to stay on the trail of the raccoon. He can't *chase rabbits* or be distracted in other ways. Invariable along any *coon trail* there will be other intersecting trails, like deer, opossums, rabbits and others. Sometimes a rabbit or deer will jump up right in front of the *coon dog.* Until the *coon dog* learns to stay on the *coon trail,* he will never make a good *coon dog.* He has to stay focused on the *coon.*

People who would grow up to maturity must stay focused on the Lord, His Word and His ways. There are notorious distractions which still work. Some of the more common distractions are a new job, a girlfriend or boyfriend, a new mate, a new sport, deep involvement in a political campaign, a new baby, a new home and a lake or beach house. One of the most successful ones I've seen is a move to a job in another city. Perhaps its only rival can be a retirement move, which means moving to a new home in *utopia* away from friends, doctors and church (and shopping). I hear the *Oh, we'll find a church*, but most of the time it turns out to be a shipwreck. I'm talking about things that often take people out of the Word and out of church. The results can be disastrous.

Burnout

Sometimes good people just get tired and worn out. Maybe they've been so deeply involved in service roles that they didn't have enough time to do anything very well. (Good people can get overloaded. The reward for good work is more work.) Maybe they found themselves misused, abused and unappreciated. Pastors are particularly susceptible to this. They give their best, work very hard, never get enough rest and wear out their bodies. Often they struggle financially and watch their mates and families struggle. Many people take advantage of them, and they face lots of pressure and mistreatment with very little appreciation. The trails of life are strewn with worn-down pastors, good men who burned out. I'm not justifying or excusing it, but simply reporting the facts.

Age takes its toll on people. Good people can become discouraged. There's always the rather pious crowd of *Christians* who are ready to say things like, *"If they were doing it for the Lord, it wouldn't matter."* That's pretty cold especially from Christians who are supposed to be compassionate. However it comes about, even strong Christians can get down and discouraged. At any junction along life's road, good people are capable of losing desire and heart. It's a sad picture, but it happens.

Let every one of us beware! Burnout is real. It could happen to you. *"Wherefore let him that thinketh he standeth take heed lest he fall,"* **1 Corinthians 10:12**. Believer, pace yourself. It's better to do a few things well than to do many things poorly. Rest enough. Keep your eyes on the Lord. Walk with God and stay close to Him by staying in His Word and in prayer.

GROWTH ACTIVATORS

That's the title of the next chapter in this book. We are about to look at things necessary for your spiritual growth and maturity. There are things you can do, steps you can take that will stimulate and enhance your growth and keep you from falling. You will find the next chapter to be very practical and specific.

Chapter 14

Spiritual Growth Activators

Robust healthy growth and development! That's the hope and heart's desire of all reasonable parents for their children. Over the years I've often been close to delivery rooms when parents eagerly awaited the arrival of a newborn. Invariably they want the child to be whole and healthy. That's far more important than the size or the sex. And, they want the child to grow up that way. No parent wants to discover a few months or years down the trail that his child is bipolar or autistic.

Even when a child is born whole and healthy, attention is required to keep him that way. If he fails to eat right, his health will quickly deteriorate. Both wholesome physical and mental development require much more than good eating habits.

Keep in mind that God draws a strong parallel between the physical and the spiritual. It is evident in the Scriptures that God wants His children to experience steady spiritual growth to maturity. This broad teaching is well summarized by the Apostle Peter. *"But grow in grace, and in the knowledge of our Lord and Saviour Jesus Christ,"* **2 Peter 3:18**. The same Bible that tells us to grow also tells us that there are practices which are essential to our growth. No one can neglect these (for whatever reason) and expect to experience a healthy spiritual growth. Thus, the following pages of this chapter examine practices necessary to spiritual growth. I call these *spiritual growth activators.* There are four general and broad categories.

PROPER DIET

Activate and stimulate your spiritual growth and maturity by spiritually eating the Word of God.

That proper spiritual food is absolutely vital to spiritual growth could hardly be expressed more clearly than in this command by the Apostle Peter. *"As newborn babes, desire the sincere milk of the word, that ye may grow thereby,"* **1 Peter 2:2**. Spiritual babies need the *"milk"* of God's Word. In this reference Peter spoke of normal, healthy babies (brephos). *"Milk"* is translated from an old Greek word and speaks simply of pure, unadulterated milk.[1] The analogy of natural milk to spiritual milk communicates the meaning of the gospel message and other truths in their purest and most simple and elementary forms.[2] What is the purpose of this simple, basic food? *Growth!* It's the same idea as seen in Paul's Colossian letter where he spoke of the body with its various parts being knit and banded together in growth because of proper nourishment. *"Let no man beguile you of your reward in a voluntary humility and worshipping of angels, intruding into those things which he hath not seen, vainly puffed up by his fleshly mind, And not holding the Head, from which all the body by joints and bands having nourishment ministered, and knit together, increaseth with the increase of God,"* **Colossians 2:18-19**. We've already seen the concept in Paul's Ephesian letter. *"But speaking the truth in love, may grow up into him in all things, which is the head, even Christ,"* **Ephesians 4:15**. The spiritual food of truth (particularly when given in love) produces growth. Without it there is malnutrition and spiritual development is hindered.

Obviously little children cannot tolerate some foods. They are not ready for steaks and jalapenos. They need milk; however, as they grow, a variety of more difficult to digest foods should be added to their diets. Likewise in the spiritual realm, babes in Christ need *milk*, but as they grow, they need stronger foods such as meat.

This is exactly what the Scriptures teach. *"For every one that useth milk is unskilful in the word of righteousness: for he is a babe. But strong meat belongeth to them that are of full age, even those who by reason of use have their senses exercised to discern both good and evil,"* **Hebrews 5:13-14**. You will recall from this text that older Christians who have had ample time to grow up are soundly rebuked for their inability to eat meat (the stronger, deeper truths of God's Word). *"Of whom we have many things to say, and hard to be uttered, seeing ye are dull of hearing. For when for the time ye ought to be teachers, ye have need that one teach you again which be the first principles of the oracles of God; and are become such as have need of milk, and not of strong meat,"* **Hebrews 5:11-12**.

You have to eat to grow. Otherwise, malnutrition and a lack of healthy maturity are certain. If you want to grow and become strong in the Lord, eat. Eat daily and don't stay on milk only, but get into the meat of the Word. The rudimentary truths of the gospel message are wonderful, and you will need them in your spiritual diet for the rest of your life. You also need to know about purity of lifestyle, holiness and separation to the Lord, how the Old and New Testaments are a perfect blend, church truths and the great prophetic messages of the Bible. You need to get hold of the authenticity and authority of the Scriptures, who Satan is, divine creation, God's purposes with the Nation of Israel, the deity of Christ and the matter of freedom of choice. Be assured that the Bible is full of great foods which will nourish, build and strengthen you. No wonder Job said, *"My foot hath held his steps, his way have I kept, and not declined. Neither have I gone back from the commandment of his lips; I have esteemed the words of his mouth more than my necessary food,"* **Job 23:11-12**. In one of King David's most beautiful Psalms, he extolled the Word of God likening it to tasty, sweet, beneficial food. *"The law of the LORD is perfect, converting the soul: the testimony of the LORD is sure, making wise the simple. The statutes of the LORD are right, rejoicing the heart: the commandment of the LORD is pure, enlightening the eyes. The fear of the LORD is clean, enduring for ever: the judgments of the LORD are true and righteous altogether. More to be desired are they than gold, yea, than much fine gold:*

sweeter also than honey and the honeycomb. Moreover by them is thy servant warned: and in keeping of them there is great reward," **Psalm 19:7-11**.

The Word of God is a growth activator. Take time for it. It is vital to your maturity.

SOCIAL CONTACT

Activate and stimulate your spiritual growth and maturity by involving yourself with the people of God in a church.

We cannot escape the fact that we are social creatures. There are a few anti-social people, but their isolation tells on them. One of the first things God recorded in His Word is, *"It is not good that the man should be alone,"* **Genesis 2:18**. God made a woman for man. We all need companionship. A wife? Yes! But the need for social interchange goes beyond husband and wife. People need people. Regardless of age, people who become isolated for extended periods of time inevitably degenerate. Babies without human contact lose their ability to function.[3]

God, who engineered and made humans, knew they would need spiritual interaction with other believers. His church is His primary answer to that need. The church is His institution, **Matthew 16:18**. Every saved person is expected to be baptized and become a member of one of His churches, **Acts 2:41**. Members in a church constitute *"the body of Christ, and members in particular,"* **1 Corinthians 12:27**. Every member is to attend the services of the church, **Hebrews 10:25**, upon *"the first day of the week,"* **1 Corinthians 16:2**. In a church members are to minister to and encourage one another. *"And let us consider one another to provoke unto love and to good works,"* **Hebrews 10:24**. That comes as Christians share their lives and testimonies, offer biblical teachings and explanations of the Scriptures. They deal together with the *hands-on* situations of life. This happens as pastors and teachers preach and teach the Word of God, older men and women teach younger men and women. You see the pattern in the early

Christians, *"And they continued steadfastly in the apostles' doctrine and fellowship, and in breaking of bread, and in prayers,"* **Acts 2:42**.

To grow and develop properly in the Lord, you must maintain regular contact and fellowship with other Christians. Social Christian contact is a growth activator.

GUIDANCE

Activate and stimulate your spiritual growth and maturity by attaching yourself to people who can guide and mentor you.

Guidance goes hand-in-glove with social contact and being an active part of one of the Lord's churches. As indicated earlier in this book, the concept of mentoring is seen throughout the Scriptures: teacher/student, mentor/apprentice, leader/follower! As people are growing up, they need help and guidance. They need someone to teach them how to study God's Word and show them how to implement the principles. They will have questions, need explanations, get discouraged, find themselves under attack and simply need a friend.

Your best place to find a guide (mentor) is in your church. There are exceptions because you may find the right person for you in the greater Christian community. You may be blessed to have several big brothers or sisters in your life all of which will help you, but almost always there will be that one *go to* person, that person you can really lean on and with whom you truly *connect*. You need a person like that in your life. That person cannot give you all of his attention, and you should not expect it. All people are mortals and have only so much time and energy. Be careful to not monopolize your mentor. At the same time don't be afraid to ask for the help you need.

Mature Christians realize that a part of God's work for them is mentoring others. To the extent of their knowledge and capacity, they are glad to do it. It grows out of the love in their hearts, and remember that love is a part of the very essence of spiritual maturity (faith, hope and charity). The Apostle Paul exemplified the heart of a true mentor when he said to young Timothy, *"Consider what I say; and the Lord give thee understanding in all things,"* **2 Timothy 2:7**. He exhorted his young disciple, *"Hold fast the form of sound words, which thou hast heard of me, in faith and love which is in Christ Jesus. That good thing which was committed unto thee keep by the Holy Ghost which dwelleth in us,"* **2 Timothy 1:13-14**. It is obvious from these words that Paul had been in Timothy's life by talking to him and instructing, giving direction and advice, correcting misconceptions and caring. Can you imagine the encouragement it was to Timothy to receive a letter like this from Paul?

Reproducing yourself in the life of another is one of those clear earmarks of maturity. The Apostle Paul was there. May you aspire to be there! As you grow you will become more and more a *Paul* to some *Timothy* in your life, just as you allow someone to invest himself or herself in you. Always a student! Yes. Forever a learner even if you have reached that point where you are investing yourself in some other person or persons. It's that wonderful cycle of which Paul spoke to Timothy (and us), *"And the things that thou hast heard of me among many witnesses, the same commit thou to faithful men, who shall be able to teach others also,"* **2 Timothy 2:2**.

We all need guidance. Never is that more the case than when we are growing from spiritual childhood into maturity. How precious to have good, godly guides at the right moments in our development. When I was a young Christian and preacher, I had a *Paul* in my life. His name was Kermit Johnson. He was not a *big name* preacher, but Kermit cared about me. He reached out to me and I took to him. We never spent lots of time together, but he was there when I needed him. He answered questions at crucial points in my development. He reached out to me, believed in me and encouraged me. I have degrees from a major seminary and a library full of books, but no person other than my dear mother has ever helped me more or had a greater impact and influence on me than Kermit Johnson. He's been in heaven for a long time, but his counsel and wisdom still guide me. I will be eternally grateful for him.

Do yourself a favor; don't wait for someone to find you. Find him. Ask for guidance and help. Make yourself available. Be a sponge. Listen a lot and be humble. Few things have the power to put you on the fast-track toward maturity like a guide or a mentor.

EXERCISE

Activate and stimulate your spiritual growth and maturity by exercise.

It's one thing to know what to do, but it's quite another to do it. In the final analysis, your spiritual growth comes down to you. The spiritual food you need is there, but you have to eat it. A social circle has been provided for you, but you have to step forward and get involved. You can know you need a mentor and that mentors are available, and yet never have one. You have to show initiative and find a mentor yourself. If you sit around and wait for someone else to do it all for you, you will be a babe in the worst sense (a nepios) for the rest of your life. You can whine, pout and blame, but that won't *cut it* with God.

You have to implement the instructions and advice that come from God's manual (the Bible) and through the guide(s) that God puts in your life. Doing it for yourself is where you gain experience. Out of experience you gain wisdom. We go back to James who says it so succinctly. *"But whoso looketh into the perfect law of liberty, and continueth therein, he being not a forgetful hearer, but a doer of the work, this man shall be blessed in his deed,"* **James 1:25**. This is implementation, pure and simple. Do it! Put the principles to work. Try them! Test them! This is where success is.

Most good jobs require *experience.* For responsible positions that pay good money, employers are looking for people who've *been there and done that.* They are not very interested in those who just read about it in a book or who stood by and watched others do it. They know that there's no teacher quite like *experience.*

God says, *"Exercise thyself rather unto godliness,"* **1 Timothy 4:7**. Don't just read about and talk about faith, practice it. Don't just preach self-control and rendering good for evil, practice it. And, there's giving and forgiving, kindness and compassion, generosity and patience, integrity and fundamental honesty, humility and holiness and this list is hard to stop. The world is somewhat of a spiritual gym where you get to practice what you preach. Just like in a physical gym, the more you exercise, the stronger and more developed you become. In fact, the Bible says spiritual exercise is far more productive than physical exercise. *"For bodily exercise profiteth little: but godliness is profitable unto all things, having promise of the life that now is, and of that which is to come,"* **1 Timothy 4:8**.

That spiritual exercise or experience pays off is well seen in **Hebrews 5** to which we have referred several times. *"But strong meat belongeth to them that are of full age, even those who by reason of use have their senses exercised to discern both good and evil,"* **Hebrews 5:14**. This verse talks about reaching *"full age."* Full age people are able to eat *"strong meat"* and *"discern between good and evil."* Who are these remarkable ones? What is the secret to their growth to such maturity? They are the ones who *"by reason of use have their senses exercised."* They've been *doing it,* not merely thinking about it or talking about it. They're the same ones James was talking about, *the doers of the work*. Is that not the heart of service? Is this not who servants of the living God are? Are not all of us who have been redeemed with the blood of Jesus Christ servants of the living God? Our job, our purpose is service, doing the work of God, exercising ourselves in godliness. Routinely! When we do it, we will be *"strong in the Lord, and in the power of his might,"* **Ephesians 6:10**. We won't be *"children, tossed to and fro, and carried about with every wind of doctrine, by the sleight of men, and cunning craftiness, whereby they lie in wait to deceive,"* **Ephesians 4:14**. Instead we will *"grow up into him in all things, which is the head, even Christ,"* **Ephesians 4:15**.

A LIFELONG PROCESS

Spiritual growth is a lifelong process. Nobody has grown all that he can. Someone has wisely said, *"The biggest room in the world is the room for improvement."* You never have to plateau. Never! Old fruit trees produce the best, sweetest fruit. Christians should be evergreens. Through thick and thin, rainy seasons and droughts and even in old age, they have the sustaining power of God to make them fruitful. Here is how King David put it. *"Blessed is the man that walketh not in the counsel of the ungodly, nor standeth in the way of sinners, nor sitteth in the seat of the scornful. But his delight is in the law of the LORD; and in his law doth he meditate day and night. And he shall be like a tree planted by the rivers of water, that bringeth forth his fruit in his season; his leaf also shall not wither; and whatsoever he doeth shall prosper,"* **Psalm 1:1-3**. Wow! *"His leaf also shall not wither"* is talking about an evergreen. Yes, all year . . . in all seasons of life! And, look at the promise of prosperity, *"whatsoever he doeth shall prosper."* No friend, you don't have to stall.

But, keep in mind what makes it this way. It's not because of who we are, but it's because of who God is. We only have the ability to grow to maturity and prosper till we die because we are connected to Him. David nailed it in that great Psalm. *"He shall be like a tree planted by the rivers of water."* Water, life-giving, life-sustaining water! Jesus is that *"living water"* of life, **John 4:10**. We cannot make ourselves great and mature. *"Not that we are sufficient of ourselves to think any thing as of ourselves; but our sufficiency is of God,"* **2 Corinthians 3:5**. Jesus said, *"Without me ye can do nothing,"* **John 15:5**. He must do it for us, and He will as we give ourselves to Him. Growth is natural, automatic spontaneous and happens when the right things are in place. You can't make yourself grow on your own. For those who are rooted in Christ, growth to maturity will occur as they *"abide in me, and I in you,"* **John 15:4**. These are the ones who grow up and *"bear much fruit,"* **John 15:8**.

SERIOUS ABOUT GROWTH

Do not misunderstand what you just read. God produces all growth that occurs in us, but He puts within our hands (our power) both the ability to activate His processes that produce growth in us and the ability to ignore or say *no* to them. That's right. The parallel between the physical and the spiritual is striking. You have the choice to eat right, exercise and take care of your body or to eat junk food, vegetate and abuse your body. God won't force you to drink the milk and eat the meat of His Word. He won't make you exercise yourself unto godliness, seek guidance or associate yourself with the right people. What you do in these cases is your choice; however, you cannot neglect His growth stimulators and still expect Him to produce steady and wholesome growth in you. You can ignore the stimulators and stunt your own growth.

To a great degree your spiritual growth will depend upon how serious you are about it. Growing up to be a mature and responsible adult is a wonderful thing, but it is deliberate and not accidental. There's a price involved and the learning process is not always easy. It takes time, diligence, concentration and considerable exercise of your brain. Sometimes life serves up some very painful lessons. Listening to an older brother or sister can be hard on the ego, especially when your weak areas and failures are in the spotlight. Most of us are not deeply in love with exercise; we prefer a more sedentary lifestyle. Exercise moves us out of our comfort zone and pushes our limits. It makes us sweat and sore. This is the way it is whether in the physical or the spiritual world. If you want to grow in the Lord, you have to make up your mind that you will do the things that God will use to produce growth and maturity in you.

Satan is a clever rascal. He's an expert at soothing consciences with good intentions. *Oh yes, I want to grow in the Lord. I want to be a truly mature servant of God. It's a New Year. One of my resolutions is to do better this year.* Wow! Now isn't that nice and noble? *Yes. I feel so good about my desire and resolution to be better. I even went down front at the invitation, fell on my knees and promised God that I'm going to be a better Christian.*

Having spent well over half a century in the gospel ministry, I have observed that sort of scenario hundreds of times. I thank God that good people get convicted about where they are in their Christian journey and want to do better, but I am more interested in follow-through. I'm wondering how this growth, this improvement is going to look. Will the days ahead produce a better attitude, response to criticism, response to adversity and greater fundamental honesty? Can we expect this person to win more souls to the Savior? Will he get into someone's life and prove to be a true mentor? What is he going to do about his temper problem, his sharp and often loose tongue, his lazy and irresponsible streak, and his unkind ways? And, what about his priorities? Does this desire to grow mean less emphasis on making money, sports and material comforts? Does it mean more attention to and emphasis on the Word of God, the family, the church, good character and integrity? Is he going to grow and do better with his money management, his use of time and the natural talents and abilities God has given him?

I have often wondered whether or not this emotional and sometimes teary-eyed Christian has really looked seriously at himself or herself. Does he really see himself? Does he know where he needs improvement? Does he know where he needs to start and where he needs to go? Does he have a game-plan, a method, some idea of how he's going to get from point A to point Z? I seriously doubt there will ever be much improvement and growth in anyone who lives in a general, starry-eyed, utopian world. Growth comes when we get serious and specific about it. It's not enough to feel a twinge of pain about where you are and experience conviction in your heart that you should do better. Conviction and good intentions are well and good, but you need to be serious enough to both (1) diagnose where you are and (2) develop a specific plan to get to where you need to be. If you are not serious, then an empty platitude (*Lord, I want to grow and do better*) is only a little salve to soothe a guilty conscience!

May every person who reads this book be serious about spiritual growth! Set your heart to seek it. Get specific. Identify where you need it most and work on those areas. Seek God's Word on the areas of your need and submit to what it says. Deliberately exercise godliness in these needy areas. Prayer allows you to seek the help of God through His Spirit who lives within you. Older brothers or sisters can give you counsel and help. Seek them out and make yourself accountable to them.

Don't lull yourself to sleep and into permanent immaturity with a general but mostly empty promise such as, *"I really want to grow and be better."* Get serious about growth. Whether or not growth and improvement happens in you is your choice.

IN CLOSING

I will leave you with a challenge and a then a beautiful but sobering poem by Rudyard Kipling. My challenge is that you **keep *your focus on the Lord.*** He seeks your welfare. Let Him grow you and use you! That's the best possible investment of your mortal life.

Here is the poem. The title of the poem is simply *If*—.

IF—

If you can keep your head when all about you
  Are losing theirs and blaming it on you,
If you can trust yourself when all men doubt you,
  But make allowance for their doubting too;
If you can wait and not be tired by waiting,
  Or being lied about, don't deal in lies,
Or being hated, don't give way to hating,
  And yet don't look too good, nor talk too wise:

If you can dream—and not make dreams your master;
If you can think—and not make thoughts your aim;
If you can meet with Triumph and Disaster
And treat those two impostors just the same;
If you can bear to hear the truth you've spoken
Twisted by knaves to make a trap for fools,
Or watch the things you gave your life to, broken,
And stoop and build 'em up with worn-out tools:

If you can make one heap of all your winnings
And risk it on one turn of pitch-and-toss,
And lose, and start again at your beginnings
And never breathe a word about your loss;
If you can force your heart and nerve and sinew
To serve your turn long after they are gone,
And so hold on when there is nothing in you
Except the Will which says to them: "Hold on!"

If you can talk with crowds and keep your virtue,
Or walk with Kings—nor lose the common touch,
If neither foes nor loving friends can hurt you,
If all men count with you, but none too much;
If you can fill the unforgiving minute
With sixty seconds' worth of distance run,
Yours is the Earth and everything that's in it,
And—which is more—you'll be a Man, my son.

---

[1] A.T. Robertson, *Word Pictures in the New Testament,* vol. 6, (Nashville, Broadman Press, 1933), 94.

[2] Albert Barnes, *Notes on the New Testament: James-Jude,* (Grand Rapids, Baker Book House, 1972), 134-135.

[3] *Wikipedia,* (en.wikipedia.org/wiki/Social_isolation).

About the Author

LESTER HUTSON served as a Baptist pastor for over 55 years. He is now Associate Pastor of Northwest Baptist Church in Houston, a field representative for the Christian Law Association, a conference and revival speaker and the author of numerous books including *Basic Bible Truths,* an internationally used soul-winning method.

www.lesterhutson.org

www.ingramcontent.com/pod-product-compliance
Lightning Source LLC
Chambersburg PA
CBHW071543040426
42452CB00008B/1094
* 9 7 8 0 9 8 3 6 8 0 2 7 7 *